A Family Tree

Diana Good

Grosvenor House
Publishing Limited

All rights reserved
Copyright © Diana Good, 2024

The right of Diana Good to be identified as the author of this work has been asserted in accordance with Section 78 of the Copyright, Designs and Patents Act 1988

The book cover is copyright to Diana Good

This book is published by
Grosvenor House Publishing Ltd
Link House
140 The Broadway, Tolworth, Surrey, KT6 7HT.
www.grosvenorhousepublishing.co.uk

This book is sold subject to the conditions that it shall not, by way of trade or otherwise, be lent, resold, hired out or otherwise circulated without the author's or publisher's prior consent in any form of binding or cover other than that in which it is published and without a similar condition including this condition being imposed on the subsequent purchaser.

A CIP record for this book
is available from the British Library

Paperback ISBN 978-1-80381-823-8
Hardback ISBN 978-1-80381-980-8

For my family

Alex, Kate, Harriet, Frances and Gloria.

Forethought

Every single one of us arrives in the world at the intersection of a double helix. There's a vast triangle of ancestors reaching back before us from our great-great-grandparents spiralling down through the generations until the helix crosses over at the point we arrive on the scene. We carry part of all those ancestors with us. That's who we are whether we know who they were or not. And parts of their life and history are carried down to the next generation who then start their own new helix.

As I get older I wonder more about the past and who came before me. Who am I? Who are any of us? We're all a mix of other families, other experiences and memories. My family comes from Lancashire, Russia and Hungary. I have Chinese second cousins and was born in Germany. When my parents married in 1955 they brought these disparate elements together. These are the threads which gave me my red hair, emotions and temper, my need to try hard, and my sense of feeling at home with people who come from somewhere else.

I had a happy and safe childhood but the generations before me had a much more complicated time and I've been affected by this, both for good and bad. I've always been interested in my family history but I've never done anything about it. Now that I'm in my 60s I want to know more and I want to share it.

I thought I had very little to go on. I went on a *Guardian* one-day masterclass about how to write your family history. It was fascinating. There were women from India and Africa who wanted their grandchildren to know where they'd come from. A woman who'd grown up in British colonial Kenya and wanted to understand why her family were there and the truth about their backgrounds. A young Chinese woman, whose grandfather had been the ruler of China before Maoism and went from being the grand man to being vilified and censored out of history. And there were many of us with Jewish emigrant grandparents.

The tutor told us that one of the classic problems with family histories is that people have far too much information with diaries, letters, photographs, objects and so on, all of it cluttering the ability to cut through and see the story you want to record. I was one of the very few who had almost nothing to go on. The tutor said that whilst this presents a challenge it also leaves you with the chance to draw on what you do remember and the pieces you have left. My maternal grandparents never talked about the past and kept nothing to remind them of it. My paternal grandmother had lots of old furniture but hardly anything in writing and my paternal grandfather died when my father wasn't even two years old. My grandparents were all cheerful people who lived in the present tense. The past was a complicated and sad place. This sadness has left significant gaps which speak volumes even if I can't fill them.

I wish my parents or grandparents were still here so I could talk to them about this but they're not and maybe if they didn't want to talk about it then, why would they now? And I also wish my parents could read this as I'd really like to hear what they think but they are very much in my thoughts and I've enjoyed thinking about them.

I have memories, some photos, wedding and death certificates, a few newspaper articles and, it turns out, a lot of letters between my parents. I've been able to fill various gaps with some extraordinary documents and that's been exciting and often very moving. I've found out a lot about double weddings and tragedy, the battlefields of the First World War, surviving Auschwitz, escaping Budapest in 1956, and orphans in Saigon.

My plan is to start with my memories of my grandparents, then go back in time to try to describe their families and background. After that I can come back to my own parents and my childhood.

I've put a chronology at the end as I've very much enjoyed discovering coincidences in the chronology with the two families experiencing major events at almost the same time with no knowledge that their paths would ever cross. Both my Russian and Hungarian great-grandfathers died in the same year, 1929, the year after my father was born; my two grandfathers were nearly at Durham university at the same time; my father was born in the year in which his parents-in-law to be (the Bentleys) got married; and my grandmother's cousins, the Ronas, escaped the Russian tanks in Hungary in the same year I was born, 1956, only the year after my mother's cousin, Dennis, married his Chinese wife, Liang Ching Ping, and they settled in Singapore.

If I stop to think who I have always felt I am, the answer is definitely a mix of all these backgrounds. Thank you to the past: the Hopes, Prescotts, Benjamins, Bentleys, Reichenfelds, Ronas and Bloodworths. And thank you to my own family, the Goods.

With my love

Diana Good (née Hope)

December, 2023

Contents

My plan is to start with my memories of my grandparents, then go back in time to try to describe their families and background using the records and photographs I've found. After that I can come back to my own childhood.

Family trees: Abbreviated version at page x and detailed versions at pages 38, 55 and 68

Chapter 1: My memories of my grandparents	1
Chapter 2: Lancashire, the Hopes and the Prescotts and the First World War (paternal grandparents)	22
Chapter 3: Russia and the Benjamins (maternal grandfather's family)	49
Chapter 4: Hungary and the Reichenfelds and Ronas (maternal grandmother's family)	63
Chapter 5: Singapore and China: Dennis Bloodworth and his Chinese wife, Liang Ching Ping, and children (my mother's cousin and family)	95
Chapter 6: My parents (Lancashire, London, and Germany)	103
Chapter 7: *Chronology* of the family showing overlaps and coincidences	123
8. Appendices: I've included in the Appendix the extraordinary verbatim journal of the liberation journey Judy Rona (who married my grandmother's cousin and who I knew), made in 1945 with a group of young women after being taken first to Auschwitz and then to the camp at Boizenburg. I've also included her daughter Mary Chait's recollection of escaping Budapest in 1956 when her family had to leave Hungary when the Russian tanks rolled in.	126
About the Author	163

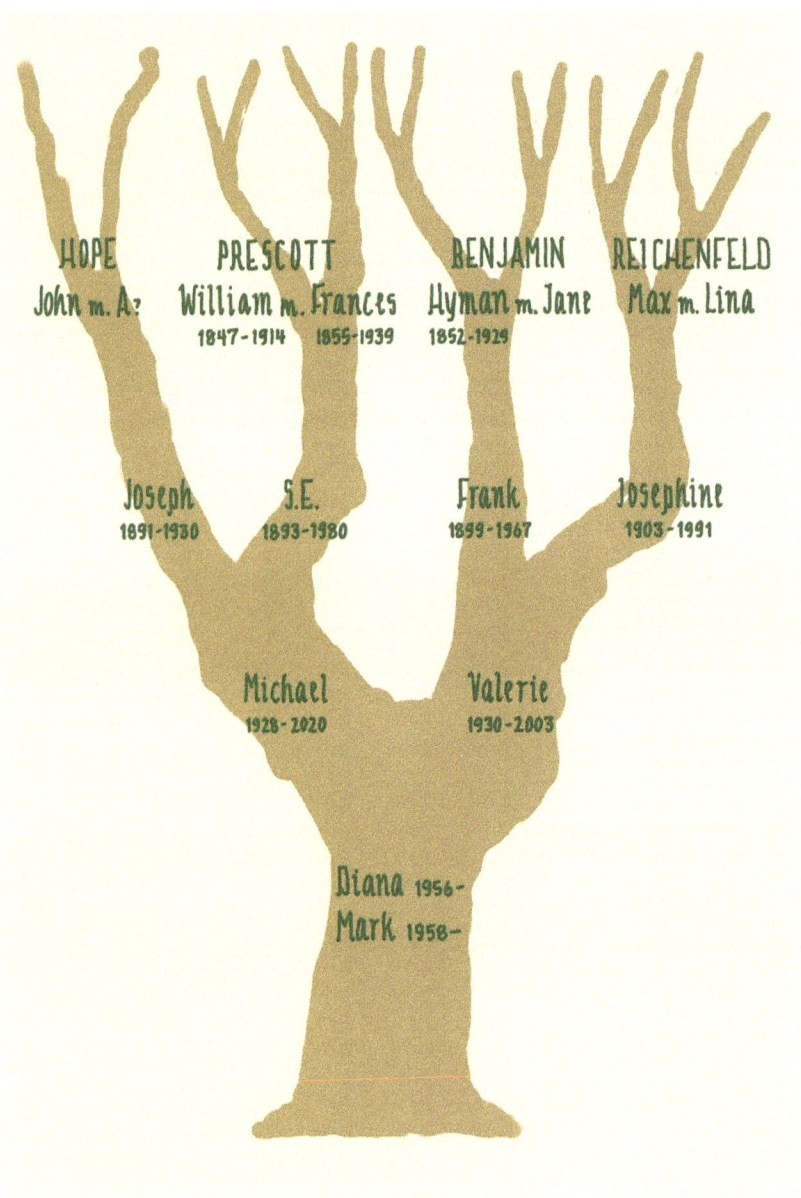

1. My grandparents

There were two weddings in the 1920s. One in London and one in Lancashire. There are no photographs of one wedding. Silence. There are many of the other wedding. The silence on that side of the family comes later.

The first wedding was in Lancashire in 1920 between my father's parents, Joseph Hope and Sarah Evelyne Prescott, who lived in mining and cotton-spinning Leigh. The other wedding was in 1928 in London between my mother's parents, the Benjamins and the Reichenfelds, Jewish refugees and immigrants from Russia and Hungary.

The Lancashire family all lived surrounded by, and in, their past, growing up in the same town, their houses full of old furniture, dark corridors with high ceilings which needed paint and proper lighting. There were no fridges (they didn't trust fridges so food lived in the larder) and no heating so there were a lot of fireplaces requiring buckets of coal and cleaning – a lot of hard work.

By contrast, the immigrant families had left their past behind, left their families and homes never to go back and losing contact with everyone there. When my grandparents married and settled in London, they rejected their Judaism and changed their name. They never wanted anything old. Everything was new.

I have fond memories of both but each side of the family has its own silences. I grew up with these gaps and I want to understand them. The silences have their own story and they matter.

The Hopes and Lancashire

Joseph Hope married Sarah Evelyne Prescott in 1920 at Leigh Parish church in Lancashire. They used to go courting on Sunday mornings before church by walking up on to the moors away from the smoke of town, its mines and mills. That was before the war. When they got married she was 27 and he was 29. She was the lucky one. Joseph was a vicar so he didn't have to fight but he did go to France as a "padre", a military chaplain. He must have read the last rites for countless soldiers who'd fought in the battles of the First World War. He will have seen terrible things but he wasn't fighting on the front so he came home.

The wedding photos outside Leigh Parish Church show the women in short 1920s' dresses but they don't look at ease in them, as if they really preferred wearing longer dresses which actually showed their figures rather than these rather plain and straight affairs. Their hats look strangely like squashed fried eggs and the closefitting cloche hats which seem to have done nothing for their faces. It was clearly a happy occasion but they have serious faces. Maybe they had to stand still too long for the photographer or maybe there was sadness in the air for all the young men who did not come home from the War. What they did not know, as the photographer lined them up, was how much sadness was to follow and would have to be endured for the rest of their lives.

The Hopes and the Prescotts were both Leigh families. On the Prescott side, Sarah Evelyne (always known to her family as S.E.) had two sisters, Frances and Maud. But to me they were all old ladies: Granny, great-aunt Frances, and great-aunt Maud, who was hardly ever spoken of as she died at 50 leaving her husband, Rupert, a widower. Joseph was one of six but I only ever knew of great-uncle Harold, one of his older brothers. Another silence. Who were the other brothers and what happened to them? I assume that some died in the war and that may well be why they weren't mentioned. So many of the young men of that generation never came back.

The youngest sister was Frances. She always wore her hair in plaits curled round over her ears like headphones, Princess Leia-style in *Star Wars*. Everyone said that she was great fun but she was one of the many women who never got married and that was another story which was never told. A great friend of the Prescott girls was Florrie Ross, known to me as Miss Ross. She was also a spinster and lived with her bachelor brother, Mr. (Ted) Ross. Their house was smaller and lighter than the other Leigh houses I knew and they were a cheerful pair. He'd been a professional soldier and had fought in both the First and Second World Wars. He'd been in the Malayan civil service which was regarded as being rather exotic.

There were two great uncles. Great-uncle Harold and great-uncle Rupert. Harold had made good. He worked as the secretary to the mine but when the mine owner died he left two mines to Harold. As a result he lived in a grand house up on the moors with huge windows and views out over the hills. He was very nice but we were never impressed as children because all he ever gave us when we visited was an apple, which he presented as he told us to be good. And he didn't impress anyone in the family when he died, leaving £10,000 to his housekeeper (a great deal of money in those days) but only £200 to my father and his sister, Mary.

Great-uncle Rupert was my favourite. He lived in a terraced house in Leigh where he always sat in the small, cosy room at the back by the fire, smoking his pipe. I loved the smell of the tobacco as we walked down the long corridor through to the back. He had a moustache and twinkling eyes as he sucked on his pipe. He always gave us a half crown – such riches that we kept them in a special box and never dreamed of spending them. And he laughed. He and great-aunt Frances would walk over for Boxing Day jollity at Granny's where we'd sit in her side room, which was rather grand with pale pink silk upholstery on mahogany chairs made more fun by the roaring fire and many games of *Happy Families*.

But, later, Frances "took to her bed". She didn't seem depressed but I assume she must have put on a good show for us when we went for tea. She had a companion and maid, Ada, who made wonderful Madeira cake and seemed to live in the cosy back kitchen. That was the nice place to be. She inherited the house from her father. He was a stonemason and must have done well because neither Granny nor Frances had to work. Maybe he had the house, Greystones, built when he was older. It was a fine Edwardian house so it was only built after he was established and had his family. The name "Greystones" makes it sound forbidding, like something out of *Jane Eyre,* but in fact it was a gentle house built on a country lane off the main road to Atherton (Old Hall Mill Lane), just outside Leigh. I recall that the road was not made up (and Old Hall Mill Lane is still not), that the house had a front garden, a big central front door and large windows looking out over the countryside. It had a big front hall and grand staircase. It must have had many rooms but all I ever saw as a child was the back kitchen where Ada had the radio on and did the baking and great-aunt Frances' bedroom, up the stairs to the left, where she chain-smoked, her fingers and face stained yellow. She once fell asleep while smoking and set fire to the bed but Ada rescued her. As a small child I found it rather frightening going to say hello. But her room was nice and light and I liked her because of the way she and Rupert had used to turn up rosy-cheeked and laughing on a winter's dark afternoon, ready for games. Frances and Gertrude Bark (who became my great friend in later life and always known to me as GB) had been childhood friends and used to go on cycling trips to the Lake District and the seaside. It was hard to see this lively young Frances in the old lady in bed but I knew she was still there and Ada was also very fond of her.

I realise that that whole generation was deeply affected by the First World War and the numbers of those who died and the mental and physical wounds carried by those who came back. I write below about my paternal grandfather, Joseph Hope, and his experience of the War, where he served as a padre. I never met him and no one else I met in Leigh ever referred to the War but it was always there.

This came home to me powerfully when I was 14 and was writing a school project about the First World War. We were meant to go and interview someone who'd fought in it and my father recommended I go and talk to Ted Ross. He was the brother of my grandmother's great friend, Florry Ross. The two of them were always very jolly and chatty and since he'd been a professional soldier who had had a distinguished military career, I had no idea that this would be anything other than a rather good chat. I remember going round to their small house in Leigh in one of the many streets lined with brick, terraced houses – line after line with no trees or front gardens. They'd invited me for tea and Florry Ross went into the kitchen to get the cake and teapot when I started the interview. Mr Ross just froze and couldn't say anything in response to my questions. When Florry came in she could see that there was a problem and tried to nudge her brother into speaking. 'Tell Diana about the time your tea froze in your mug, Ted,' she suggested but he couldn't do that either. I remember being shocked that, over 50 years later, Mr Ross just could not bear to say anything about his experience. I've now seen his obituary which shows that soon after he went to university the War broke out and he joined the Royal Fusiliers. He first served in Egypt and the Middle East and was then made battalion adjutant in the Battle of the Somme. He later became a colonel and won the Military Cross. He joined the Colonial Administration Service and held senior positions in Malaysia, India and Ceylon and fought in the Japanese invasion of Malaya in 1941/2 and, after the fall of Singapore, escaped to Sumatra, after which he fought in India. He must have seen so many terrible things. Maybe he couldn't talk about any of them but the Battle of the Somme was clearly too shocking to begin talking about. Leigh was full of men like this and women who had never got their son or husband back.

But as a child my experience of Leigh was of jolly times. Games were a major part of my experience of visiting Leigh. I remember playing *Monopoly* with Granny when we teamed up because we were both doing so badly. We held out for ages with just Whitechapel and Old Kent Road, charging £5 rent to all who landed on our guest houses and managing to shake lucky dice each time we needed to dodge the scary lines of hotels which the others had waiting for us along the pink and red stretches of Pall Mall and Whitehall, the Strand and Trafalgar Square. Of course, Park Lane and Mayfair did for us in the end but it was exciting and we laughed a lot.

In my mind's eye I can picture Leigh very well. It was a mining and cotton-spinning town where most of the population worked in either the cotton mills or down the coal mines. My father was a keen photographer and took several stirring photos of the back streets and industrial scenes along the Bridgewater canal. Granny and great-aunt Frances lived in the middleclass areas with bigger houses but the bulk of the streets consisted of narrow terraced houses with back-to back yards.

A FAMILY TREE

We lived in neighbouring Bolton, another mining and cotton-spinning town. Bolton was a boom town in the 19th century and by 1929, Bolton had 216 cotton mills and 26 bleaching and dyeing works, which made it the largest cotton production centre in the world at that time. I remember every time we drove home from our holidays we would drive over the moors and look down on the high chimneys of the mills and the smog of Bolton, and my parents would pull a rather long face and say, 'Home again.' In fact, we lived on the edge of town surrounded by fields but I remember that the number of chimneys belching out smoke was an impressive sight.

Gertrude Bark (GB) wrote about the Leigh she and my grandparents grew up in in the 1890s in the history of her parents' recipe book, which I edited and published after her death as *Around the Kitchen Table*. GB was my great-aunt Frances' friend from primary school onwards. They were lifelong friends who obviously had fun together. GB's father was a bookkeeper for the mines and wrote her mother's recipes down in his beautiful copper plate writing. She wrote, *"You can see straight away where this book came from – coal dust smudged all the way through, some pages very black, colliers – a lifetime in this small exercise book. What sort of a place were these recipes living in from 1890 onwards? Coal mining, cottonspinning, silk weaving Leigh with the Manchester ship canal and barges passing through by cottages"*. She told me that when she got married she was given a pair of miners' lamps which I can recall always hung by her bedside. She wrote, *"These were the sort of men who asked my father, "What does 'er want for 'er wedding?" My father nearer to tears than I'd ever believed, asked me and I said, 'A miner's lamp – one they've used in the pit, not a shop new one.' And my father told me when he told them what I'd said I wanted coal black Tom said without hesitation, 'Er mun have a purr!' So I did. I went down to the wharf to thank them. 'Think nowt on it lass... Dun ye like it love? It were mine.'"*

I love to read the Lancastrian accent GB liked so much and was very insistent we needed to get right in the writing up of her memories. I grew up with that accent and it makes me feel at home and safe. GB described how, when she was very ill with tonsillitis, one of the miners brought a kitten to the kitchen door for her. He came upstairs to her room and *"held up in his great scarred hands a wonderland of a black kitten"*. As he went downstairs she heard him say to her mother, *"'Er'll be aw reet now, and don't you worry Misses Wilim, 'er's aw reet now.'"* GB writes that when she woke up, she felt well and happy again.

My father writes about the accent as being known as "Lanky". He writes of the miners who would squat on their haunches outside their homes and the old women who would wear shawls over their heads and shoulders and wear clogs on their feet. They would say "tha" instead of "you" and "thi" instead of "yours". He grew up saying "lurry" for "lorry", "book" and "bath" with a short "a". If I ever had a Lancastrian accent, and I suppose I did at school, I lost it pretty fast as did my father when he joined the army. But he still used to say, "Don't worry" like "sorry", rather than "wurry" and I've always pronounced salt as "solt" (also like "sorry") instead of "sawlt". I can hear our cleaner and babysitter Mrs Partingon's voice saying, 'I'm that vexed with yer I could shake yer,' but then she'd soften and say, 'Bless you, luv.' I love that Lancashire voice, it makes me feel at home and I can't think of Lancashire or the Hope family without hearing that accent. So there's still a tiny remnant in my accent of the voices I heard as a child until we moved south when I was nine.

It's important to understand that the towns are surrounded by high moors and wild, beautiful country – another world from the chimneys and mills below. Sarah Evelyne and Joseph used to meet on Sunday mornings to walk up on the moors. I think they must have had to catch a bus to get there. It's easy for me to imagine my grandparents striding off up on the moors when they were courting and also gazing down on the mills. At weekends we often used to go up Rivington Pike where there's a tower standing at the top of Winter Hill, standing at over 1000 feet above the land below. Once you'd clambered up there, first through the trees and then out on the open moor, the wind would blow so hard that, as a small girl, I could lean back against the wind and not fall over. We'd hide behind the tower and then bob round backwards into the wind trying to steady ourselves and then spread our hands out wide, lean back into the wind, and imagine we were about to be carried away up into the sky and float out over the reservoir and fields below. In winter, the reservoir would freeze over and the icicles were the longest I've ever seen. It was grand! And our dog, Gus, would love tearing off hallooing into the distance, chasing another of his imaginary rabbits.

Granny lived with Mary in a semi-detached Victorian red brick house called Broomfield, 138 St Helen's Road – a fairly busy main road. This is where Granny moved after her husband's death with my father, two year old Michael, and Aunty Mary, only eight months old. The house was just around the corner from Pennington Hall Park which had a grand old house, a pond and a very small and rather straggly zoo. I have a vivid memory of the house. It was only shortly before my father died that I discovered that I lived there as a two year old and that after that there was such a big fall out that my parents had no contact with Granny for four years although they lived only twenty minutes away. The rupture was significant but that story will have to come later on.

The house stood on the corner of the main road and an unmade lane called New Barn Lane. This meant that although the front of the house was fairly narrow (only one room and the corridor deep), it went back a long way with garden all along the side of the lane and also at the back so the side rooms had a garden view through dark privet hedges, but the corridor, staircase and landing did not. Usually we went in through the garden and to the side door by the kitchen after parking in the bumpy side lane, but sometimes we'd go in by the front door facing the main road behind the privet hedge. On the right there was the living room where there was always a fire burning and where Granny sat most of the time.

On the left by the front door was the gong with the lion's head in brass and the umbrella holder, an art nouveau tall china pot in orange, both of which we still have, and the coat rack which we used to have at Aberdeen Park. I liked arriving at the front door and it was because I was fond of these items that I asked for them when Granny died. The brass lion's head with the "bonger" to call people to meals has a very worn-down and illegible inscription. I've always understood it was a gift to Sarah Evelyne Hope from the grateful congregation of her husband's parish.

The corridor was tall, dark and scary so you wanted to scamper down that as quickly as possible, into the pink and mahogany parlour room where we played *Happy Families* at Christmas. Further down the corridor, at the back, there was the jolly kitchen which had a large table we all sat round, the larder and the big dresser and cupboard which we also had at Aberdeen Park.

Daddy always made us laugh when he told us about what a terrible cook Granny was and how she once made a "surprise" pudding. This was a sponge pudding which once cooked was turned upside down onto the plate which then revealed its surprise ingredient such as a slice of pineapple. Mummy used to make us castle pudding, which had syrup at the bottom, but we were allowed to pour extra golden syrup over it from a great height, standing on our chairs and watching the golden syrup curl down from our spoons all the way down to the pudding. We loved doing that. But the pudding my father remembers was different. On this occasion in Leigh, Granny dished it out and it had a strange bright yellow thick layer at the bottom, which my father and aunt eyed with suspicion. Granny always used to say, in her Lancashire accent, 'Get something into you,' when it came to any fussiness about food and she will certainly have told them this when they started to fiddle about with their spoons. She said it was full of good stuff and to eat it up. As they tried to get through it and she dug deeper into the pudding for her own helping she found the lid of a tin which was labelled "Boot Polish". It was this which had given the pudding its "surprise" element, both in terms of colour and taste!

Another story of a memorable pudding was blancmange (which used to be very popular but which I hated, a nasty milky blobby kind of pudding which wobbled a lot on the plate). My father told us about an occasion on which the blancmange was being passed round the table. When it came to Mary, Daddy's sister, she knocked her funny bone on the table as she reached for it, which caused her to pass out but all anyone else was aware of was that she gently laid her head sideways into the pudding and lay there as if asleep. My father thought this was terribly funny but this didn't make me any fonder of the pudding as and when presented with it.

At the very back of the house was the scullery with sinks for washing dishes and clothes. It was cold. Outside was the garden, the potting shed and the garage in which lived the old Morris Minor.

Before the war Granny had a live-in maid who used the small back bedroom and the outdoor toilet next to the washroom outside the back door. On Mondays they had a washer woman who came and hung out the washing to dry either in the garden or the kitchen where there was a large clothes rack you could pull down from where it lived up near the ceiling. After the war the cost of living went up and Granny could no longer afford the help.

Going upstairs was a scary business as it was very steep, with a big drop down through the bannister, and was barely lit with what seemed to be one light bulb at the top which cast terrible shadows up and down the stairs which moved as you walked. After a long climb, the corridor split either taking you either straight ahead past the bathroom to Mary's room at the back or turning right to the front where Granny's room was and where there was a cupboard full of her hats which my brother Mark and I used to like trying on. Before you got to Granny's room you passed another bedroom which was bare, with the ceiling collapsing. It was not a nice room and I've had nightmares about sleeping in there when I was very little. I never told my parents this until Daddy was in his 90s and he then told me that it had been his bedroom and that he'd always been scared of it. How strange that these moods in a room can last and haunt.

My father said that he never liked the house. He said it was dark since it faced east and it was very long and narrow. But he always said he had a happy childhood there. He wrote *"Mother was warm, kind and considerate. I had plenty of friends and lots of toys. Pets included a spaniel called Peter who I loved and a tortoise called Jimmy"*.

Granny had what I called a waffly nose, twinkly eyes, bird's nest hair and a cosy body. Mary and she would come down for Christmas to Kenley where we lived when we moved south.

Once they famously got lost in the Morris Minor and failed to turn off the M6 onto the M1 for London and managed to drive all the way to Bristol down the M4 before they realised they weren't going to London. They phoned us from a phone box in Bristol to explain that they were going to be late. After that incident they used to catch either the train or the bus.

As in her own home, Granny liked to sit by the fire and snooze. I remember one Christmas my brother Mark and I dared each other to look at the large pimple she had on her chin with a big hair growing out. We got quite close when she suddenly opened her eyes and laughed and we realised she hadn't been asleep at all.

I remember Granny always being fun but it was hard-earned and now I know just how much. I always knew that her husband died when my father was not even two and his sister not even one but I did not know until much more recently that my father had an older brother who died when he was very small. In fact, not even my father knew about the other baby until he was much older and maybe not until he came to bury his mother. There's so much that a child doesn't know and so much that isn't spoken about in families. But this would explain why it is that after the many wedding photographs there are so few photos after Joseph's death.

The Bentleys: Russia, Hungary, Yorkshire and London

My mother's parents, Francis (always known as Frank) Bentley and Josephine Richfield, married in London in 1928. He was born Francis Benjamin and her family's original name was Reichenfeld. He moved south from Yorkshire and she left the bedsit she'd shared with her sister on Carnaby Street. There are no photographs of the wedding and soon after they changed their name, rejected Judaism and became atheists. What happened?

During their married life they moved several times from central London, to Bourne End, on the river, during the war, and then to Brentwood in Essex where he ran a TB hospital for children, to Hampstead Garden Suburb, and finally to Wimbledon. I have photographs of us all in the house in Hampstead Garden Suburb but I don't remember it. The only place I recall is their flat in Wimbledon. Grandpa wanted to move there so that, when he died, as he knew he soon would, she would be left somewhere that was easy to manage. Never any regrets or nostalgia. The past was not something to cherish or hold onto.

When my husband, Alex, and I bought our first house, a 19th century terraced house in Stoke Newington, and filled it with second-hand old pine furniture, Granny Bentley wanted to know why on earth we wanted an old house full of "all these old things", saying that she'd only ever wanted everything new, nothing old, nothing from the past. And her modern flat in Wimbledon near the common made that very clear. The furniture was comfy and new. There were just four rooms with big sliding modern windows, a lift, a garage for the car and definitely good heating. There was nothing from their past at all, just a few photographs of her and Frank when they were young adults, no trace of Hungary or Russia which seems strange since Granny loved her long window ledge collection of tiny figures and animals. But they were all collected while on holiday. They did not come from the past.

And that is why trying to piece together that past is difficult.

My grandmother: Jo Bentley

Granny would always say, 'Hello, darling!' on arrival. She'd then talk at great length about what she'd been doing. After a while she'd say, 'What's news with you?' And then she'd carry on talking, barely drawing breath for any reply. She was proud of her blonde hair as a girl in her 20s and had a photograph of herself on the sideboard in the living room.

She never ever talked about life before her 20s but she did like to talk about her sister, Marguerite. There were five children: Tibor (who had minimal contact with the family and made it clear that he wanted nothing to do with them), Rosalie (older sister who I did know), Marguerite (the favourite sister and great friend), Josephine (my grandmother) and Alfred (who I did know).

Rosalie was the eldest. When I knew her she lived in a flat in St John's Wood with her rather yappy little Chihuahua. She had

My grandmother, Jo Bentley in her 20s

rather grand manners, wore quite a lot of makeup and smelt of powder. I think she played a lot of cards and had quite a social life, if dwindling as she grew older. I don't know what happened to her husband and Granny didn't get on with her but her son, Dennis Bloodworth, was a huge favourite with Granny, my mother and Aunty Janet. Indeed, there was a rivalry as to who saw most of him and had spoken to him most recently. Luckily, Dennis was a very nice man and knew how to get on with everyone and make everyone feel special. He had not had a happy childhood at home so he spent a great deal of time living with my grandparents and he was as close as a son and brother to them all. Dennis was very fond of Granny and always brought out the best in her but he also knew her well. I remember at her funeral he made a wonderful speech in which he said that he knew that she could be difficult but that whenever he turned up at her house and received the classic Jo welcome – the big hug, eyes lit up and a big smile as she said, 'Hello, darling!' – he would feel safe and welcome. He knew that she had a big heart.

Dennis married a Parisian girl but that didn't work out and after a while living and working in Paris as a journalist he was posted to Singapore by the *Observer* as their Far East correspondent and he became a very distinguished writer on China and all matters in the Far East. He married Ching Ping, or Judy, who was Chinese and had had to flee during the Long March. They couldn't have children but they adopted her sister's three sons. They had been left orphans. They always lived in Singapore where my parents visited several times, but I never went. I did meet them in London. Of the three sons, Dominic, Bosco and John, the younger two came to live in England and we saw them quite often until Bosco, who was a chemist and lived in Deptford with his Chinese wife, Alice. They left to go back to Singapore after a few years and not long after that John moved back too

I also met Alfred, who was the youngest. He lived in Saltdean near Brighton on the south coast in a bungalow built on the rolling South Downs – pleasant but all covered with lookalike bungalows which made you feel the loss of the grass and the swoop of land down to the sea now that it had all become concrete. He was happily married (for the third time) and had two sons, Melvin and Tom. We only went there once with Granny. I think they got on well enough.

I'd like now to be able to ask Granny about them all and their childhood. We did talk years ago and Granny once gave me the very few photos she had of her and Grandpa's families as, she said, I was the one who showed most interest in the family. But she never offered any information about her childhood and I didn't pursue it. But what she did tell me about was her favourite sister, Marguerite. They were great friends and the photos show that they had fun. There are several of them on holiday, and showing various boyfriends.

I can hear her voice telling me the story of what happened.

"We lived in a rented room in Carnaby Street. Our mother had been a dressmaker and we got work modelling clothes in Dickens and Jones, which was just round the corner. None of the clothes were ready to wear then so ladies would come in to the shop, watch girls like us model the clothes, decide which

*Josephine and Marguerite Reichenfeld
(my grandmother and great aunt)*

they liked and then the dress or coat or hat would be made to their size.

"Marguerite was the pretty one, petite, dark hair, lovely face and figure. I had blonde hair but I was gawky in comparison; bony jaw, big nose, taller and noisier. We did absolutely everything together. We had no money but we laughed. We slept in the same bed, shared our clothes, modelled together and dated boys together. I remember us coming back from a night out one evening and asking Marguerite to throw me my rag (which was my nightie) and she said, 'But, darling, it really is a rag,' and we laughed and laughed so much. I loved her very much. We were good-time girls. If you modelled you weren't considered to be very proper and we had fun with boys. We once went to Le Touquet for the weekend with two Irish boys. It was fun but they weren't serious. We wanted to find two boys who would want to marry us and look after us. So one day we dressed up in our best on a Sunday and went to the Waldorf where they did tea dancing. There was a band and you could take turns dancing with a different partner and then have tea and cakes in between dances. There were two young men there who'd come down from Yorkshire for the weekend. They were so nice. Frank was a doctor and Bernard was a dentist. They were brothers. I think I got the handsome one, Frank, but Marguerite was very keen on Bernard. It was very romantic and we met them there several times. They used to come down on the train and we'd have a date to go out with them.

"We went on seeing them for five years. We loved it but one day my mother said, 'Jo, it's been five years and they're never going to ask you to marry them. You're both getting older and you need to find someone else who will take you seriously.' So I explained that we couldn't marry them because they were Jewish. Their family had left Russia to escape the pogroms. The whole family were practicing Jews. They would never be allowed to marry us. My mother suddenly looked very serious and said, 'Girls, you need to sit down and I'm going to explain something to you that I've kept secret.' She explained that we were in fact Jewish. She'd come from a gentile Hungarian family. She'd converted to marry their father. They had five children and moved to London. They left everyone they knew. Life wasn't easy in London either and shortly after they arrived the father left, abandoning his wife and children. So my mother decided then that she would reject Judaism and refused to bring the children up Jewish but since it goes from mother to child it meant that all of us were in fact Jewish.

"We went straight to the post office and sent a telegram to Frank and Bernard saying, *We are Jewish!* A telegram came straight back saying, *Meet us at Euston off the 6:10 train.* So we both went to the station and the two of them jumped off the train, both carrying engagement rings, saying, 'Marry us.' They had to go straight back to Middlesbrough as they had work the next day. We planned a double wedding. I thought that Marguerite and I would be able to live close together, have children together, and share everything right into our old age."

But, Granny went on to say, only three days before the wedding, Marguerite complained of a spot behind her ear and started to get a terrible headache. She had meningitis and died only two days later. My aunt's notes say that it was Marguerite's last wish that the wedding should go ahead. Frank and Jo did get married but it was obviously too sad for any celebration. I don't know where the wedding took place, or if anyone else came. This explains why there are no photographs of the wedding. I suppose it must have been a Jewish wedding but Granny didn't want to talk about that. In her 80s she told me that if she had any wish that could come true she would wish for Marguerite to be alive and to be her best friend now. She wanted the girl who laughed at her "rag" back. She'd wanted to be old ladies together, both laughing at what life chucked at them. Bernard went on to marry another woman called Marguerite who I sensed my grandmother never liked.

These photographs of Marguerite and Granny show them both looking very pretty.

Sisters: Marguerite and Josephine

I've now learned a lot more about some of Granny's Hungarian family (who I knew) and I'll describe below her cousin's survival of the Holocaust, Judy's journey home to Budapest from Auschwitz and their later escape over the border when the Russian tanks rolled in, in 1956. I don't know anything much about my Russian grandfather's background. That really is an unknown and not something I've ever heard anyone talk about. Again I've found out more than I knew as a child and I write about that below as well.

My grandfather: Frank Bentley

I'd like you to imagine my grandfather. He had a thin face with a long nose, round glasses and kind eyes. He always liked the joke of all the letters he put after his name: MRCS LRCP (1922) MB BS Durham (1922) MD (1924) MRCP (1925) DPH (1928) FRCP (1937), RHS (all medical qualifications except for the last which was Royal Horticultural Society, which, as a gardener, he was proud of). And he always used to make us laugh by putting entire chocolate biscuits into his mouth, much to Granny's disapproval, which encouraged him even more, of course.

My grandfather, Frank Bentley

He was a distinguished doctor who specialised in TB in children and helped to eradicate it. We knew that he'd caught TB and this had weakened his heart permanently. The Royal College of Physicians' obituary describes my grandfather's distinguished medical career, describing the many jobs he had, from the Newcastle Royal Infirmary to Great Ormond Street, the Medical Research Council and London County Council. He published a paper in the *British Medical Journal* in 1940, which was the first comprehensive paper on mass radiography in the UK and was the result of his work with a number of soldiers who had joined up at the outbreak of the Second World War. The period of his career which he was most proud of was being medical superintendent at Highwood Hospital for Children in Brentwood working on TB in children.

In 1954 he wrote "Tuberculosis in Childhood and Adolescence", which the obituary states "achieved a worldwide reputation". He taught postgraduates at Great Ormond Street and undergraduates at the London Hospital and Guy's. I knew he was distinguished and had worked, successfully, to eradicate TB in children but I had no idea it was quite this impressive.

The obituary finishes on a much more personal note,

"In 1928 he married Josephine Lily, daughter of Max Reichenfeld, a restaurant owner, and they had two daughters. An asthmatic childhood and continued ill health during his professional life had imposed a great deal of restriction on him, but in spite of this he was gregarious, liking good company, films, theatre, good books and good food. He was an erudite and witty conversationalist. He had many hobbies, being a keen gardener in early life and later an untiring traveller and an excellent photographer. After his enforced retirement he became an expert croquet player – defying his medical advisers – and died at Hurlingham, which he had come to love so much, after a pleasant game".

I remember the day Grandpa died and what Granny told me about it. He was 67. He and Granny were playing croquet at Hurlingham Club where they were keen members. I remember Granny saying that it was a beautiful day and he'd just completed his turn. She told him what a beautiful shot he'd just made and then she went out to play her turn leaving him sitting on the bench to watch. But when she finished her shot and turned back he was just sitting still in the sun. He'd died. She later found his diary in which he wrote that he knew that his heart would not last out so he'd taken drugs which would keep him going but one day he would go out like a light, and he did.

Mummy was very fond of her father and I remember when the call came. It was a weekend and we were all at home. We were out in the garden when the phone rang. Mummy went in to answer it and I remember hearing the most terrible groaning cry. It was a shock and the first death I was aware of. I was 9 and my mother was only 37 so it was a shock. My father wrote a condolence letter to Granny which Mummy must have kept from granny's papers. He wrote, *"Frank was a good man… He was unfailingly considerate and kind. Whatever his own troubles he was always ready with sympathy, encouragement, and warmth for others. Above all he had a generous spirit which made the world, or rather wherever he chose to be, a more interesting and pleasant place. Frank had another quality. He was an open, honest man… In Lancashire they call such a person genuine: it is the highest praise"*.

The fact is though that my grandparents, for some reason, never approved of my Lancastrian journalist father as they didn't think that he was good enough for their daughter and this always put a great strain on the relationship. I think Daddy meant what he wrote in this letter and, as I say, Mummy always liked her father a lot but things were always much more difficult with Granny, who always made it apparent that she preferred her younger daughter, Janet. Relations certainly got worse after Grandpa's death, rather than better.

At my parents' wedding: Frank and Jo Bentley, great-uncle Harold and S.E.

MY GRANDPARENTS

This is a photograph from my parents' wedding in 1955, the year before I was born. On the left are my London Russian and Hungarian grandparents, Frank and Jo Bentley. On the right my Lancastrian grandmother, S.E. Hope, with her brother-in-law, my great-uncle Harold, since her husband, Joseph, had died 25 years earlier. No one looks as if they're pleased to be together. They all look stiff, except for great-uncle Harold who seems at ease, but then he had become a millionaire by then. All of them are very smartly dressed. All are professional and self-made with parents who had been, from left to right, a Russian immigrant trader; a Hungarian immigrant restaurant manager; and a Lancashire stonemason. The father of the bride and the father of the groom were both the first in their families to go to university and both went to Durham, studying medicine and theology respectively. So they really had quite a lot in common but London disapproved of my father, a journalist for the *Leigh Journal* (definitely not a professional). I suspect that Lancashire also felt ill at ease even if more certain of their origins.

In the background of the photo, the standing figure is John Scrivins (who I always knew as Uncle Bob), my father's best man and subsequently my godfather. John Scrivins married Jean who, much later, became my stepmother when she and my father married after my mother had died.

Now I'll go back in time and write about my great-grandparents and the families and places my grandparents grew up in using research and documents rather than memories. They are rather different.

2. Lancashire: The Hopes and the Prescotts

My paternal grandparents were Joseph Whittle Hope and Sarah Evelyne Prescott. They married on 21 October 1920 in Leigh Parish Church where he had been the curate. By then he had become the curate of Lancaster Priory Church. He was 29 and she was 27. On the marriage certificate both fathers are referred to as "gentlemen". I have a copy of the *Leigh Journal* article where the wedding is described in great detail including exactly what was worn and itemising every single wedding present and the donors.

The article is headed "Wedding of former Leigh Curate", and reports that, *"The bride, who was given away by her uncle, Mr. W. Chadwick, was charmingly gowned in white satin beauté, lined with pink georgette, trimmed with hand embroidery and pearls. The full court train was fastened at the shoulder and waist with sprays of orange blossom. Her bouquet was of pink rose and lilies of the valley, and she wore a diamond and platinum brooch, the gift of the bridegroom... the bridesmaids were dressed in turquoise blue satin beauté, trimmed with gold lace tissue and wore veils of blue net, with headbands of blue and gold".* I'm impressed. In truth, I've always looked at the wedding photo below and thought that although they were clearly dressed in the 1920s latest fashion in short skirts it looks pretty frumpy with the bride and bridesmaids wearing a poached egg type of headdress which looks more like a shower cap than anything else. Perhaps it's the black and white photography letting the side down. They must have looked rather special.

It was obviously a happy day. *"After the ceremony, a reception was held at the Co-operative Hall, over 50 guests being present. The honeymoon is being spent at London and Bournemouth, the bride's travelling costume being of navy blue, with lemon and*

My grandparents' wedding: Sarah Evelyn Prescott and Joseph Whittle Hope

white panne hat." The boat had been pushed out but this was very much a local wedding for family and close friends along with my grandfather's fellow clergymen.

It's the list of wedding presents (set out in full detail in the article) which I find gripping. Fancy publishing item by item for the public to read and such a contrast between the grandeur of some of the presents and the very simple gifts of many. Every single present is listed but these ones stand out:

"Bride to bridegroom, study desk (and we know that he gave her a brooch)

Mother of bride, piano (and I knew that dark mahogany piano which stood in the pink drawing room down the corridor from the living room)

Father and mother of the Bridegroom, antique writing desk

Congregation of Leigh Parish Church, mahogany clock (which is the clock we now have in the living room at Preedys Farm) *and pair brass vases*

Mr. H. Hope, Chesterfield and easy chairs (this is Great Uncle Harold, who was also the best man, being Joseph's brother)

Mr. S. Hope and Miss Philipson, gong (is this the gong with the brass tiger's head which stood by the front door and which I now own? But I thought that was given by the congregation to their rector's wife, Granny, in thanks. The trouble is I can't read the much-worn inscription on the gong.)

Mr. and Mrs. W. Smith, supper cloth and d'oyleys (these were GB's parents and from much more humble background than the Hopes and Prescotts, the father was bookkeeper for one of the coal mines).

The Rev J. and Mrs. Bardsley (Lancaster), silver inkstand (she appears again below and not in a good light)

Miss Oberend (Rhos-on-Sea), luminous bedroom clock

Miss G. Smith, Bruges etching" (This is GB, who became my much loved old lady friend and who, as we will see below, had, only the previous year, been to Bruges and visited the battle fields and taken some extraordinary photos for a small album. I think she probably bought this etching while there).

There are several simple gifts such as *"Mrs S Smith, Old oak candlestick"*, *"Mrs France, pair of pewter teapot stands"* (both of these are relatives of GB's) and *"Miss Prestwich, tray cloth"*. But there are also some significant gifts, such as *"The Rev and Mrs Rubie (Lancaster), electric stove and saucepan"*, and here's a mystery, *"Mr and Mrs J Coop (San Francisco), cheque"*. Who were they? They're the only people who aren't very local although there are a couple from Bournemouth, Birmingham and Cardiff.

We can leave them going on their honeymoon at this point and find out more about their lives and families.

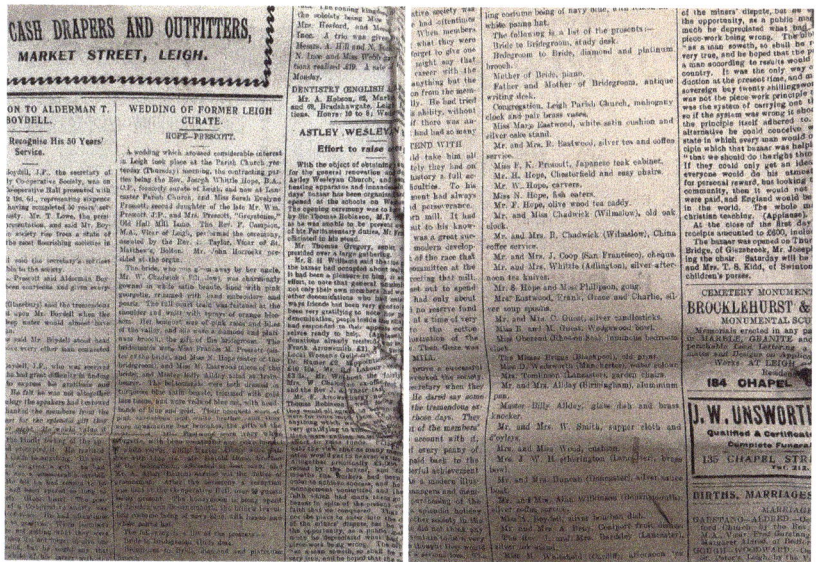

Leigh Journal covers my grandparents' wedding in Leigh Parish Church

Joseph Whittle Hope 1891-1930

The Rev. Joseph Whittle Hope (always known as Joe) was the grandfather I never knew. He was a vicar and clearly a fine man who was liked and admired. My father writes that he was once stopped in the street and asked by a stranger if his father was the Rev. Joe Hope and when he said yes, the stranger simply said, 'He was the finest man I have ever known,' and with that he walked off.

He is a significant figure in the family but he died when my father was two years old. My father says his only memory is of him "striding home from the church to the vicarage about one mile away down a long straight road". He often had a dream in which this memory was repeated. In the dream my father is a small boy and is standing at the gate waiting for his father to come home but although he could see him coming up the lane he never gets there. When my father started his autobiography he found that he got stuck when he started to think about his early years as he kept remembering his mother crying a great deal, and no wonder.

It must have been terrible for Granny. Joseph had survived the war and been one of the few of his generation to come home. They had a very happy wedding but ten years later he died of appendicitis in the days before penicillin when nothing much could be done. He suddenly suffered terrible pain and was taken to Preston Nursing Home but they didn't diagnose appendicitis or operate in time so he died of a burst appendix. How grim. He was only 39, leaving his widow with two very small children and she will have lost the house too since it was a vicarage and they will have had to find a new vicar. The funeral took place only three days after his death on 29th October 1930 at St Anne's Church, Woodplumpton, where he had been vicar. After that, Granny went back to Leigh to live near the rest of her family.

Joseph and Sarah Evelyne together in happier times.

My grandparents: S.E. and Joseph Hope

The church has a window in his memory which was unveiled and dedicated at St Anne's Church, Woodplumpton on 18th September 1932. I have the order of service from which I can see that the opening hymn was "Praise my Soul the King of Heaven" which, strangely enough, was Mummy's school hymn and one of her favourites, was my school hymn and, because of all that, was the first hymn at our wedding. I certainly didn't know that it had been sung on this occasion as well.

Mark and I went with Daddy to visit the church (which is nearer Preston than Blackpool) in 2013 and attended a service in the church. We were touched and impressed that, when Daddy explained to the vicar that he was Joseph Hope's son, his eyes lit up and he immediately said, 'But we have a window in his honour and we always teach the Sunday school children all about the First World War because he was a chaplain in France.'

"In honour of the glorious Resurrection of our Lord Jesus Christ and in loving memory of Joseph Whittle Hope, M.A. Hon C.F. Died 26th October 1930, aged 39, Vicar of this Parish 1927-1930."

Joseph studied theology at Durham University and was ordained in 1915 as part of those studies. He was a padre in the First World War. By the time of his wedding to Sarah Evelyne Prescott, Joseph had already been curate of Leigh Parish Church (which is how he met his future wife) and was by then curate of Lancaster Priory Church, now a cathedral. After that he became the vicar of St Mary's South Shore, Blackpool before becoming the vicar of Woodplumpton.

Granny was a widow for over 60 years and I don't remember her ever talking about him so I have to piece Joseph Hope's life together from other sources. Of course, my father was also curious to know more about his father and I can see from his papers that he did quite a bit of research trying to track down his role in the First World War, with some success. My father wrote, *"I know almost nothing about the Hopes. We used to visit my grandmother Hope in Bolton once a year for tea but she never visited us. Like grandmother Prescott and great-aunt Clara she was a very dignified, very large, worldly wise church going lady. She always*

Stained glass window in memory of Joseph Hope at Woodplumpton Church, Lancashire

wore a long black dress buttoned up to the neck (where she wore a narrow ruff) which went right down to her shiny black boots on quite high heels. Like grandmother Prescott she always had whiskey available for visits by gentlemen". My father wrote that he didn't remember many conversations with grandmother Hope but that he recalled her saying that she was brought up in a very religious household and that they went to church twice on Sundays.

We know that my grandfather's parents were John Hope and A. Whittle and that they lived in Bolton (where I grew up). They had five children of whom Joseph, born in 1891, was the third: Arthur, Harold, Joseph, Frederick and Nellie. The only one I knew was Harold (who I have already described as becoming very wealthy after he was left the cotton mills he had previously worked in as the secretary but who only gave us an apple when we went to visit, much to our childish disappointment). My father explains that, of all the other Hopes, he also only knew his Uncle Harold and that although Leigh, where my grandmother lived, is only seven miles from Bolton, before buses, trams and cars, these communities lived very separate lives. Either way it was only ever Harold who showed any interest in my grandmother and her children and it was he who came to my parents' wedding, standing in as the father figure in place of Joseph.

In my father's papers there's a newspaper clipping of the death of a Mrs. E Hope who was 96 when she died and "probably the oldest woman in Atherton". It states that she married Mr Arthur Hope of Atherton in 1866, presumably my grandfather's oldest brother. *"Mrs Hope had a wonderful memory and could recall the great changes that had taken place in her long life, and the manners and customs of her younger days. She could vividly describe her visit to London for the opening of the Great Exhibition at Crystal Palace by Queen Victoria and the Prince Consort".* So they kept a newspaper clipping of the eldest brother's widow but there was never any reference to either her or him.

I know that Joseph went to Durham University to study theology and was ordained there in 1915. It's very odd to think of him being at Durham at almost exactly the same time as my other grandfather, Frank Bentley, was studying medicine also at Durham University. Frank was a "prizeman" in 1918 and graduated in 1922 so they won't have overlapped but it was close.

Even today there is a partnership between the Anglican Church and Durham University. Durham is, apparently, one of the few places in the world where vocational training is offered to those who want to become Church of England ministers. The university specifically mention St John's Hall, as the college where the course is studied and that is where Joseph was ordained from in 1915 as a deacon and as a vicar in 1916.

Conscription only started in 1916 and clergymen were not required to join the armed forces but Joseph joined the Royal Army's Chaplain Division. My father wrote to them to make enquiries and they sent him a note of his record card but it contains sparse information. It states, *"Joined the Royal Army's Chaplain Division on 13.11.1917 from Vicarage Square Leigh, Lancs. He was then 26 ¾ years of age, and single; he was medically fit and described as "moderately evangelical, bright like Campbell". And on 18.12.1917 he was sent to France with BEF.*

After the war he was made Honorary Chaplain to the Forces (HCF) in 1919.

He served with the 34th division under Lt Colonel J. Shakespear

He was ordained deacon in 1915, priest 1916 at Manchester, St John's Hall, Durham-BA. Curate at Leigh from 1915-1920, then Curate of Lancaster from 1920 -1924. From 1924 to 1928 he was at Holy Trinity, South Shore, Blackpool and in charge of St Mary's. In 1927 he became Vicar of Woodplumpton, Blackburn, and remained there presumably until he died. His last entry in Crockford's is in 1930."

My father always said that his father was at Passchendaele, one of the most terrible battles of the War. But I'm puzzled by the dates as I can see that although there was fighting around Ypres from 1914 to 1918 the battle of Passchendaele was over (in early November) by the time Joseph seems to have arrived, according to the Army's records. It does seem strange that he was "sent to France" only the week before Christmas so perhaps the date in the records is wrong but there will still have been a lot of men in hospital and a great need for moral and spiritual support. And there were plenty more battles in 1918 including at Amiens, Cambrai, Mons and Albert.

Lyn Macdonald, the First World War historian, wrote a book, *They called it Passchendaele,* based on the eye witness and firsthand accounts of 600 men. Daddy was informed that on page 209 there was a photograph of the padres of the 34th Division, which includes Joseph Hope so it seems clear that he was there.

The records show that a great many Lancastrians fought at Passchendaele. It seems that that it was both Lancashire (East Lancashire, South Lancashire, Loyal North Lancashire and Lancashire Fusiliers) and Yorkshire regiments that bore the brunt of the fighting at Passchendaele. Since Joseph became vicar of Leigh in 1915 there must have been many deaths of young parishioners. I think there must have been a point when he thought he should go out there to join them and help them cope. I've been puzzled about the timing but I imagine firstly that there was a lot of bureaucracy to be gone through and transport probably took a long time to organise.

The notes explain that he served the 34th Division under Lt Colonel J. Shakespear. I see that the 34th Division was an infantry division raised in 1914 to fight in the trenches in France and Belgium. Colonel Shakepear was born in India and had served both as deputy commissioner in Assam and political agent in Manipur. He was 54 when he was sent to France. It must have been a far cry from the hills of India. As it was from the normal lives of the young men he commanded.

The military chaplains were known as padres. They weren't allowed to wear uniform or to fight so they weren't in the fighting but their role was very demanding. They were required to provide last moments of comfort to the men who were dying even out on the battlefield. They had to deliver the news of the death of fellow soldiers to the men, write to the families and visit those families on return to England. They also had to minister to those awaiting death following a court martial. But worst must have been administering the last rites to men who were dying in no-man's-land

and having to identify the remains of troops they had seen on a daily basis, and attempt to create a marked grave. In that landscape of death, with guns booming and men dying of grisly wounds, it must have been horrifying work. And it was dangerous sometimes under active gunfire. In all, 168 padres died in the war.

Passchendaele was a tiny village five miles from Roeselaare (where our friends, Kris and Mieke, live) and on a ridge to the north east of Ypres. Ypres had been a battle ground since 1914 but the third battle of Ypres (known as Passchendaele) has the reputation for all that was most grim and futile about the war. The numbers are shocking, with total deaths in that five-month-long battle amounting to half a million. It became a symbol of the mud, madness and senseless slaughter fought over a very small piece of ground. The British claimed victory on 6th November 1917 but there was more fighting after that and then, in 1918, the battlefield was abandoned only for it to be evacuated the next year.

I have no letters home from Joseph and if they did exist they would probably have been the standard stiff upper lip letter which did not reveal the horror of what they were living through. To understand we have to read what was written later.

Lyn Macdonald based the title of her book on a line in the poem by Siegfried Sassoon, "Memorial Tablet". Sassoon was not at Passchendaele as at the point of the war he was in England after a court martial and signed off for nervous collapse, but he fought before and he knew the utter horror. He became a focal point for dissent within the armed forces and profoundly disagreed with the continuation of the war. He wanted the brutal truth of what men had suffered to be understood by a public that was largely ignorant of the horrors of the trenches. He records with anger and bitterness the horror and pointless sacrifice of the hell of the war:

"I died in hell—
(They called it Passchendaele). My wound was slight,
And I was hobbling back; and then a shell
Burst slick upon the duck-boards: so I fell
Into the bottomless mud, and lost the light."

The *Encyclopaedia Britannica* gives an impression of what it was like. "The explosion of millions of shells, accompanied by torrential rain, had turned the battlefield into an apocalyptic expanse – a swampy pulverized mire dotted with water-filled craters deep enough to drown a man, all made worse by the churned-up graves of soldiers killed in earlier fighting.

Conditions for the soldiers were horrifying. Under almost continuous rain and shellfire, troops huddled in waterlogged shell holes or became lost on the blasted mudscape, unable to locate the front line that separated Canadian positions from German ones. The mud gummed up rifle barrels and breeches, making them difficult to fire. It swallowed up soldiers as they slept. It slowed stretcher-bearers to a literal crawl as they tried to carry the wounded away from the fighting through waist-deep muck.

Passchendaele would be remembered as a symbol of the worst horrors of the First World War, the sheer futility of much of the fighting, and the reckless disregard by some of the war's senior leaders for the lives of the men under their command."

Lyn Macdonald's book makes for tough reading. Just one quote from stretcher-carrier Private F Hodgson of the Canadian Field Ambulance gives the impression of what it involved. "It took six of us at a time to get one stretcher out through the mud... the walking wounded had been coming in all day. It was a terrible job carrying in the dark – almost impossible... He was very frightened the wounded boy. He said to me, 'Am I going to die, mate?' I said, "Don't be stupid, fella. You're going to be alright. As soon as Heinie stops this shelling we'll have you out of here, and they'll fix you up OK. You'll be back across the ocean before you know it.' The shelling eased off and we picked him and started off again. He died before we got him to the dressing station. On the way back we passed the remains of our No. 1 squad. There were nothing but limbs all over the place. We lost ten of our stretcher-bearers. Hell was never like that".

The book also describes that by the 1920s, Ypres had become the first place of mass tourism in history with tens of thousands of people travelled there in cross-Channel steamers to Ostend and then pouring onto trains and out again at the shabby wooden sheds that served as temporary stations. They were nearly all women in search of the places where their sons, husbands, nephews, cousins had died. They were pilgrims rather than tourists. "A whole generation of young men lay buried under the Flanders mud".

This is fascinating because in my father's papers I have a small photo album which my Great-aunt Frances kept of the trip which she and her great friend (and much later my dear old lady friend) Gertie Smith (who later married and became Gertrude Bark and known to me as GB) made in 1919 to the battlefields. The front page contains this note: *"Our trip to Belgium and France. 1919. Snaps taken by Gertrude Smith"*. I can't tell if my grandmother went out as well or not but I expect she did. There's a photograph of three Edwardian ladies in the distance. I don't know if it's them or not.

I discovered from my father's notes that, after the War, Joseph Hope stayed on with his regiment, the Loyal North Lancashire, which served in the occupation of the German Rhineland around Bonn, which is strange given that this is where my parents ended up living and where I was born. So I don't know whether Joseph was still in Germany when the friends made their trip to the battlefields or not. Whether my grandmother and Joseph were already seeing each other or not, I assume they would all have known Joseph Hope when they went on the trip as they will have gone to Leigh Parish Church where he was the curate. Perhaps he went with them?

GB will have wanted to see something of where her beloved cousin, Dick, died. In her book of recipes, GB describes that he signed up when the war started in 1914. He went to say goodbye to his headmaster. The headmaster recalled how her cousin saluted him with, 'Goodbye, sir,' turned, saw the cane with which he'd been given "six of the best", saluted it and said, 'Goodbye, old friend,' and went. The book contains the recipe for Dick's favourite chocolate cake. He wrote to her considering the possibility of being wounded and arriving during some starshine night in Manchester. *"All the way from the trenches"* he said *"and be sure to have a chunk of your chocolate cake in your pocket for me"*. He never came back. He was 19.

This little album is an amazing record. It must have been incredibly courageous for these young women from Leigh to have made the journey so soon after the end of the war. GB was a nurse during the war but none of them would have been abroad before and would not have understood the level of devastation they were going to witness. There were, and still are, tens of thousands of bodies which were never recovered as well as the vast war cemeteries.

The photos taken by GB show the boats at Ostend, the ruins of Ypres and the village by the Battle of the Somme (where her cousin Dick died) as well as the wreckage of Albert, Amiens and Cambrai. The Battles of Albert, Amiens and Cambrai took place in 1918 so perhaps Joseph was posted there after Passchendaele. GB's photo of the Cloth Hall at Ypres completely matches Lyn Macdonald's description:

"Four years of war turned Ypres into a ghost town. Not a leaf grew on a tree. Scarcely one stone stood upon another. From the battered ramparts the eye swept across a field of rubble to the swamplands beyond. The jagged ruins of the Cloth Hall tower, still pointing an angry skeleton's finger at the sky, was the only evidence that a town had ever stood there."

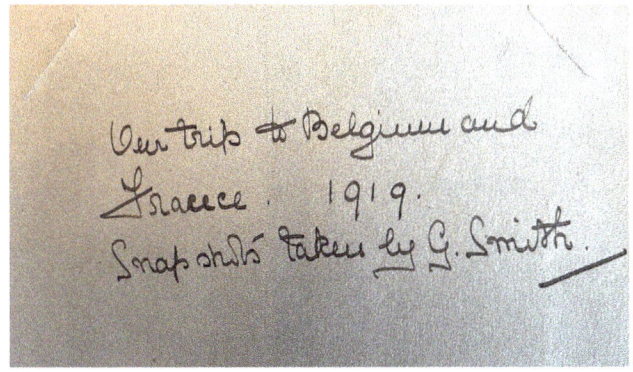

Photo album of trip to the WW1 Battlefields snapshots taken by G. Smith (known to me as "GB")

Ostend with British Ships in harbour 29 August 1919

Ypres and Albert in September 1919

These are GB's snaps but this is the more famous image taken at the time at Passchendaele.

Passchendaele Battle Field

The Prescotts, Leigh Lancashire

My grandmother, Sarah Evelyne Prescott, was born on 27th April 1893 at 133 Leigh Road, Westleigh (her birth certificate refers to her father, William Prescott, as a "retired stone mason") and died 29th January 1980. She was the middle of three daughters: Maud, the eldest sister (married Rupert Eastwood, children Peter and Mary, Maud died 1946), and the youngest, Frances, 1895-1978.

Granny's parents (and my father's grandparents) were William Prescott, born 1847, died March 1914, whose father, Richard, was a bricklayer, and Frances (Fanny) Chadwick born 1855 and died 1939. Fanny's father, Richard, was one of nine children born in 1819 and died in 1889. I have their wedding certificate which shows that the wedding was at Leigh Church on 14th April 1887.

It's very interesting to see how both the Prescotts and the Chadwicks advanced themselves. While the marriage certificate of William Prescott and Frances Chadwick shows William's father, Richard Prescott, as a "Bricklayer" and Frances' father, Richard Chadwick, as a "Mason", a generation later at my grandparents' wedding, the wedding certificate then refers to their fathers as "Gentlemen".

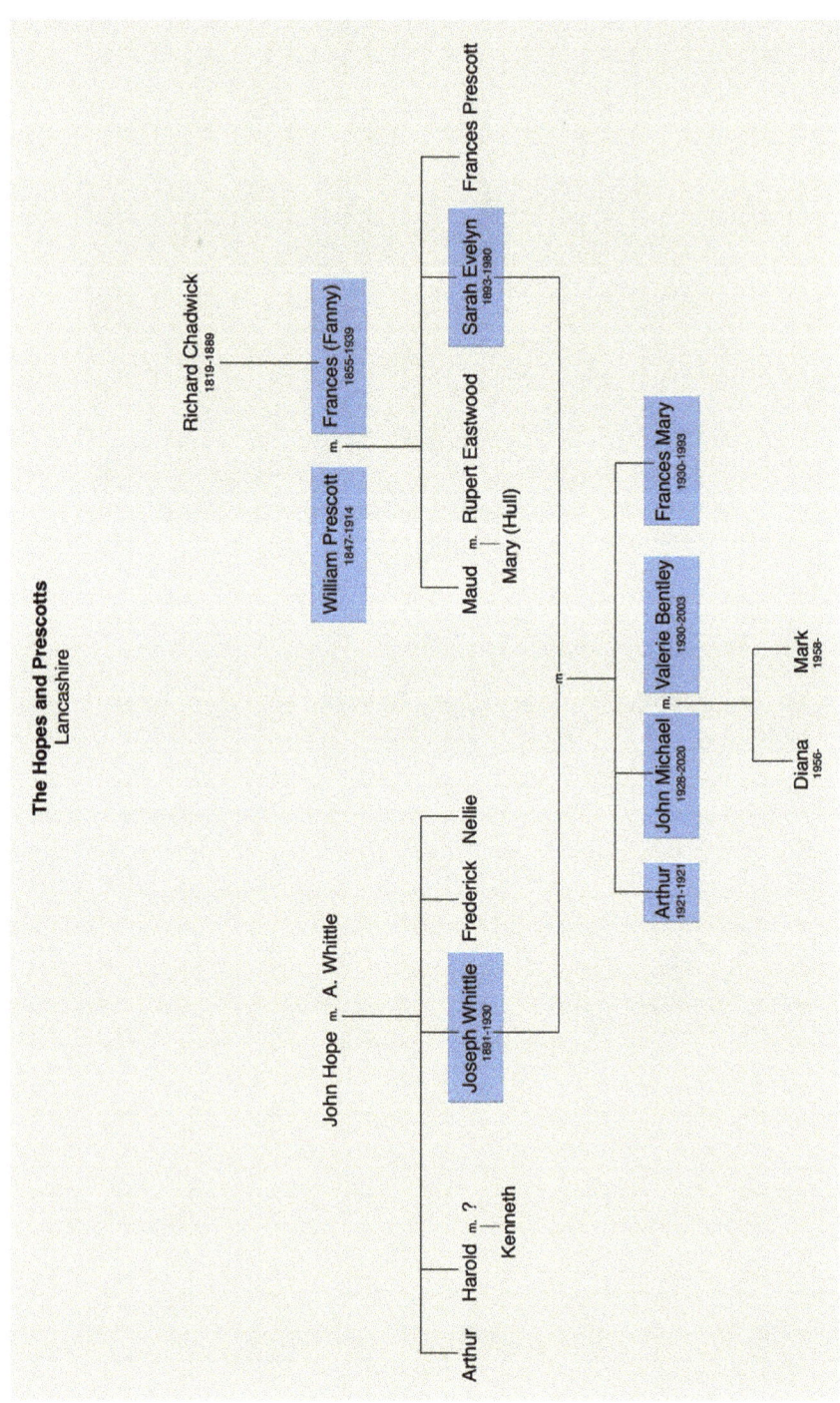

William Prescott

I have a charming small book which has the 1856 dedication to the very young William Prescott for good attendance at the National School, Leigh. It contains his own entry which shows that at aged nine his writing was beautiful but his spelling very poor. Of course, the prize was for good attendance rather than for good work. His note seems to say, *"Steal not this book for fear of shame for hear you see the honersname"*. The book itself is titled *Lucy, or The Housemaid and Mrs. Browne's Kitchen*, clearly thought to be suitable reading for a nine-year-old.

William Prescott became a stone mason merchant and married Frances Chadwick. They had three children: Alice Maud (who married my great-uncle Rupert), Sarah Evelyne (known as "S.E.", my grandmother) and Frances Mary (my great-aunt Frances).

My father knew his granny Prescott and wrote, *"She also was large and wore a long black dress with a frilly neck piece and shiny black boots"* like his other grandmother. *"However, she was quite jolly and wore a silvery chain around her waist on which she carried not only a set of keys but also a small penknife which she used to peel and cut up an apple every tea time"*.

William Prescott was clearly successful (my father assumed he made grave stones, *"a steady business"*) and made enough

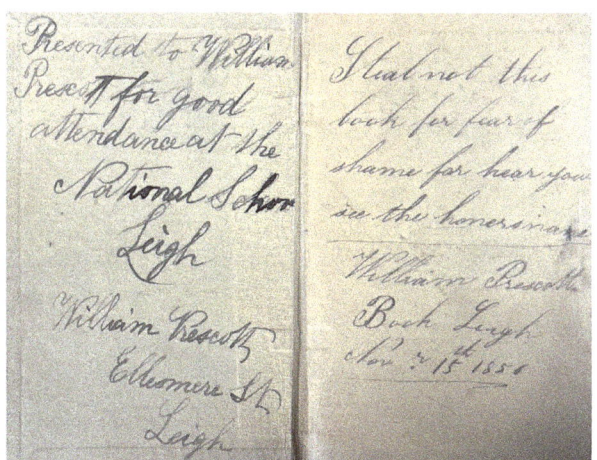

1856 prize given to William Prescott, my great grandfather

money to send all his daughters to public (boarding) schools which was very unusual at the time – SE and Frances to Abbot's Bromley. He died in April 1914 (buried in Leigh Cemetery) leaving £32,286, which must have been quite a lot of money and certainly resulted in none of Granny, aunt Frances or sister Mary having to work.

As a widow, Frances Prescott moved from 73 Leigh Road to Greystones, Old Hall Mill Lane, Atherton, the house her daughter, my great-aunt Frances, inherited and which I knew and visited as a child. Frances Prescott died in July 1939. Strange that my great-grandfather Prescott died just as the First World War started and that his widow, my great-grandmother Prescott, died just as the Second World War started.

Maud married Rupert Eastwood who was a cotton broker and served in the war in East Africa where he caught malaria, from which he suffered with shivering and perspiring bouts for the rest of his life. He was a good tenor and he and great-aunt Frances used to play the piano and sing of a Sunday afternoon to entertain everyone and I can remember that too.

Great-aunt Frances never married. This photo shows the look she kept even as an old lady with neat hair in coiled plaits.

Great-aunt Frances as a young woman

The Chadwicks

My great-grandmother Prescott was born a Chadwick. There were many Chadwicks and they were clearly wealthy. I have a copperplate list of the nine children of John and Mary Chadwick who were born between 1811 and 1838. Interestingly all of them lived to a good age. My grandmother's grandfather was Richard, the fourth child.

List of the Chadwick children 1811 to 1853

My father knew his grandmother Chadwick, who also always dressed in long black dresses and was formidable. Here is one of the grandmothers (I don't know whether she is Prescott or Chadwick, but most likely Prescott) in the famous long black dress walking at the seaside with my great-aunt Frances. I like the way she looks even more formidable by virtue of the double image.

My great grandmother (Prescott or Chadwick) with Great-aunt Frances

I have some marvellous photograph albums with beautifully painted plates and many photographs of ladies in grand dresses and one young man in uniform, back from war, looking as if he'd just come back from the Crimea. It's clear that these are photographs of the Chadwick family but since, bar one, there are no names and no other documents, I have no idea who they are. (There's a lesson here which is we should always name our photos even if it's obvious to you who they depict because future generations will have no idea).

From the Chadwick album

The William Chadwick, referred to in the photograph below as "My Beloved Husband", seems to have been the youngest of the Chadwick children in the list and my grandmother's uncle, who died in 1905.

Daddy writes that *"one of the tales his mother told was that there was a Chadwick fortune in Chancery, derived from a 17th century Bristol merchant but no one had successfully claimed although many had tried"*. It's interesting looking at the family papers as on this side of the family there are a lot of documents relating to probate, wills and estate duty, correspondence with lawyers and cemetery fees. I assume this is in part because my father had to deal with the deaths of each of his mother, his aunt Frances

From the Chadwick album

and his sister, Mary, and that included information about William Prescott's. There is nothing of this kind in relation to Joseph Hope or his family but then that all happened when Daddy was a baby so perhaps it makes sense that he had no such papers. But it also shows that the Prescotts and the Chadwicks were established families, had more to leave to their descendants, and had family lawyers. This is in marked contrast to my mother's side of the family where there are no such documents (save for the will which Jo Bentley changed twice, another story which we will come to).

Amongst all of the many legal documents I've found is a letter from Mary Hull (my father's cousin) in February 1980 after great-aunt Frances died. Mary was the only daughter of Kenneth Hope. She was the granddaughter of great-uncle Harold who was very wealthy but had scandalised the family by reputedly leaving everything to his housekeeper. Great-aunt Frances left the house, Greystones, to her maid, Ada Blackburn, and, in the event of Ada's death to my aunt Mary, leaving the balance to be split between her nephew (my father) and her nieces (my aunt Mary and Mary Hill). Mary Hull was clearly not impressed and she didn't appreciate having to pay any of the relevant expenses. I never got the impression that there was much love lost between Daddy and Mary Hull and now I can see why from the tone of her intemperate letter.

"Dear Michael,

With reference to your letter of February 20th, I should have thought that your sister would have enough from Aunt Frances' estate to pay for this flummery without taking from my share.

As for your approaching Marsh's (the family solicitors charged with sorting out the estate) *without consulting me, I consider it gross impertinence. I am advising them that under no circumstances will I agree to this expenditure.*

Yours,

Mary Hull"

My father told me that it related to an argument over a memorial for the three sisters. The vicar had proposed a new altar for Leigh Church but Mary wasn't having it. In the end, Frances was buried in Leigh Cemetery where her father and mother were buried.

I think it all goes to show that money was important in this family. They may not have been exceptionally wealthy but they were definitely very comfortably off and the fact is that none of Granny, great-aunt Frances or aunty Mary had to work.

I know nothing of Granny's childhood save that she and her sister, Frances, went to the same primary school as GB. At secondary school, each of the three Prescott sisters (Maud, Sarah Evelyne and Frances) were sent off to boarding school so they definitely didn't share schools after that, but Frances and GB stayed lifelong friends.

In the papers I have there is a dear little scrapbook album which seems to have been given to Frances in 1907 by Mary, who must have been a friend. Her family and friends have written or drawn something over the next few years and it conjures up an image of girls having fun. It includes a page of the Prescott family's signatures: William, Frances (the mother), and the sisters, Maud, Evelyne and Frances; an entry signed E.P., who I think must have been my grandmother (Evelyne Prescott); a page of friends including Gertie Smith (later GB); an excellent drawing of "Christmas Shopping" copied I assume from a magazine, signed by G.S. (Gertie Smith again).

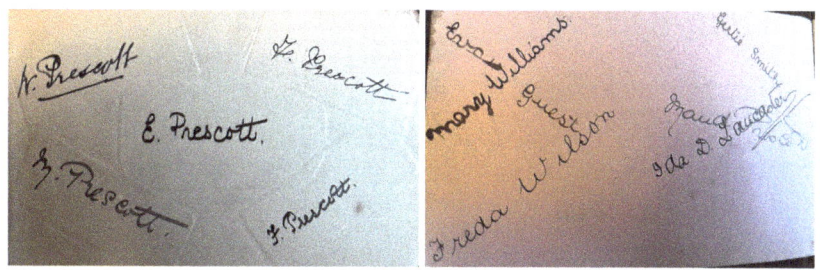

My grandmother's notebook with Prescott family and friends' signatures

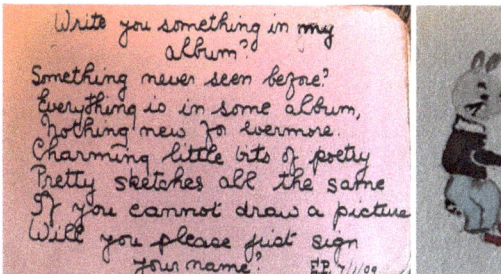 

More from Granny's childhood notebook

"Christmas Shopping" drawing by Gertie Smith (known to me as GB)

I think of my grandmother as being a jolly person who lived comfortably but she did have to deal with a lot of sadness. One of the things, which even my father only found out about decades later, was that before him his parents had had another baby, Arthur Leigh Hope, who died not long after he was born. Joseph Hope was then working in Blackpool where he was sent by the vicar of Lancaster. There had been an argument because after Joseph completed his curacy at Lancaster, he was offered the living of a church but this involved having to move from their nice house on the edge of the Priory Close to a rather poor part of town. My grandmother refused to move from their house and as a result of this row, the bishop of Blackburn offered Joseph a living in Blackpool where they then moved. Clearly there were very poor relations between my grandmother and the vicar of Lancaster and his wife, the Bardsleys, who are recorded in the article announcing their marriage in the *Leigh Journal* as having given them a silver inkstand as a wedding present. My father's papers contain the following chilling letter which Mrs Bardsley sent to Granny's mother after the death of the baby (I assume that after the death, Granny went to stay with her mother).

"Dear Mrs. Prescott,

I have been away from home for several weeks and only just found your letter awaiting me on my return home last Friday evening. I am indeed sorry to hear that Mrs Hope's baby only lived so short a time, it will be a great disappointment to her but I am afraid as long as the world lasts children will have to suffer for the faults of their father's and wives for those of their husbands – I hope your daughter is now strong again.

Yours truly, A.M. Bardsley."

This letter must have intruded on so much grief it's hard to imagine how thoughtless and cruel a letter this was and it can only have been kept because Granny and her mother were so hurt and cross. They then waited seven years before having another child and that is why there is such a long gap before my father was born in 1928. And after that they rapidly had another baby, my Aunt Mary. Months later, Joseph died leaving Granny a widow with two tiny children

My father knew nothing about the fact that there had been a previous baby until he was much older. It must have emerged, if not earlier, when Granny died and was to be buried in the same grave as her husband, where the inscription shows the name of the baby boy. The papers and fee from the cemetery include the charge for adding the name of Sarah Evelyne Hope to the two other names already on the stone, Arthur Leigh Hope and Joseph Whittle Hope. I don't know why they were all buried in Heaton Cemetery, Bolton, rather than in Leigh. I can recall Granny's funeral. We drove in a big black limousine following the hearse through the streets of Leigh and all the way to Bolton. People would stop and take their hats off and show respect as we drove by. In fact, in the car there was affectionate laughter as we remembered the jolly times with Granny but I had no idea of the sadness of this first baby's death. I remember the somber cemetery and the coffin being lowered into the ground but of course at that point the headstone had been removed so I didn't see the names then and my father didn't tell me until a few years before he died.

When I urged my father to write his memoirs, he got on quite well until he reached the age of almost two when his father died and then he got stuck. He explained that all of his childhood he had not thought it was that bad a thing not to have a father; so many fathers who had come back from the war were never the same with shellshock or injuries. But the more, as an adult, he stopped to think about what had happened, the more he realised how awful it must have been and the memory of his mother crying a lot came back to him.

Later, my father's sister, Mary, became very depressed. I know she had wanted to marry GB's son E.W. (Ernest William) but for whatever reason, GB did not approve and that was not to be. Daddy told me that this happened while he was already in Bonn so he was never very clear about what had happened or why, but it clearly shook Mary badly. She had a job at the BBC in

Manchester but left that and then never worked again. She lived at home with Granny and there were, sadly, several occasions on which she despaired and took too many sleeping pills. Each time my grandmother found her and called the ambulance and Mary pulled through. I used to like my aunty Mary with her pretty blonde hair and she could be very funny, but she smoked a lot and I remember once being frightened when they came to stay with us and she locked her door and wouldn't come out and everyone was fearful of what they would find when the door was finally opened. In the end, she died peacefully in her 60s in an old people's home.

3. Russia and the Benjamin family

My grandfather, Frank Bentley, died when I was eleven and I remember it very clearly. I'd never known anyone die before and I went to the funeral. Granny was dressed in black and was very sad. She was only in her mid-60s and it had been a shock but she was determined not to cry and I remember her being very annoyed that it was her older sister, Rosalie, who "let the side down" by weeping.

I don't think that Granny and Grandpa had the easiest of marriages. I recall Granny telling me about difficulties during the war. And in one of my mother's letters to my father, when he was working in Germany while they were engaged, he had come to visit the Bentley family in Brentwood and it clearly went badly. In the letter she sympathises with his awkward meeting with her parents and wrote that she could just imagine Grandpa saying "the first ten years of marriage are the worst". It must be something he'd said before.

But my memory is of them getting on very well in their old age and doing everything together. In their flat in Wimbledon, the sofa and chairs had the covers they had embroidered together and the rug was also a co-creation. Mark and I went to stay for a week or more when I was seven in 1964. I only later discovered Mummy had had to go into hospital for a miscarriage but we didn't know about that and we had fun. They took us to see *Mary Poppins*, which had just come out, and to Hurlingham Club where they were members and there was a swimming pool and mini golf. And Grandpa made us laugh by eating entire chocolate biscuits in one gulp, much to Granny's dismay.

Frank Bentley was born Francis Joseph Benjamin on 28th December 1899. His father was a Russian Jew who I had always thought fled from Russia during the pogroms at the turn of the 19th and 20th centuries. Frank was the youngest of five children. The eldest was Horace (born in 1891) followed by Judith

A FAMILY TREE

(b 1893), Cyril (b 1895), Bernard (1897) and then Francis (1899). Beyond this there is very little family information about Grandpa's family: no birth, marriage or death certificates and no recorded memories. It seems to be the case that there was a rift in the family after he married my grandmother, Jo, in 1928. Soon after that my grandparents changed their name to Bentley and rejected Judaism. It's Grandpa's family where I thought I had least information and the silences seem to be the loudest. So it's been interesting trying to piece together his story.

I don't recall either of my grandparents or my mother ever talking about his family and the family records are very vague. So I have to separate out what I grew up believing and have imagined since and what I've since discovered is actually correct. I'd always understood that his family were Russian Jews and that they had fled because of the pogroms and settled in Yorkshire. But there are several areas of confusion: Where did my great-grandfather come from, what was his name and who was he married to?

First, where was he from? I understood him to be a trader but I didn't know where from although I'd assumed Odessa. In the late 18th century, Russia acquired territories in Poland and Lithuania (the Russian Partition) that contained large Jewish populations. In these conquered territories, a new political entity called the Pale of Settlement was formed in 1791 by Catherine the Great. Under the tsars, Jews were only allowed to live in the shtetels ("little towns" in Yiddish) in the Pale of Settlement. This means that in the 19th century, any Russian Jews had to live in one of modern Ukraine, Belarus, Eastern Poland, Moldova or Lithuania.

My great-grandfather is described in the family tree my aunt Janet made as Isaac Benjamin, a *"White Russian, peddler, money lender"*. The term "White Russian" refers to the people who lived in Eastern Ruthania, today Belarus. So that indicates that he came from Belarus but did he stay there? Or did he move at some point to Ukraine or another part of the Pale?

Since I've been so short of facts, I've allowed my imagination to wonder. In my mind, Grandpa's family went on the most extraordinary journey as refugees. I imagine it being grim having to abandon their home after attacks which had perhaps sorely affected members of their family, and travel in fear with five children to the complete unknown.

I did research into the pogroms. Tsar Alexander III is recorded as having a "ferocious hatred of the Jews" because of the assassination of his father. This made Jews easy targets of pogroms and anti-Jewish riots. The pogroms went on throughout the history of the Pale but there were bad ones in the 1890s and then particularly devastating ones from 1903 to 1905. Because I'd imagined my grandfather, the youngest of the five children, having to escape when he was only five or six, I looked first at the huge pogrom in 1905 in Odessa when thousands of Jews were assaulted and killed after the mutiny of the sailors on board the battleship *Potemkin*. The population protested in support of the sailors against the tsars but the anger was rapidly turned against the Jewish population resulting in quarter of a million Jews leaving the country. Most went to America but many left for England.

I know that the Benjamin family arrived and settled in Middlesbrough, Yorkshire. But then how did they get there? Boats must have left Odessa but they would have gone out through the Black Sea and then the Mediterranean in which case Portsmouth would have been a more likely place to disembark than Yorkshire. So did they in fact travel overland to Poland and sail from Gdansk out through the Baltic and across the North Sea, in which case Middlesbrough would have made more sense? Or were they in fact not from Odessa but from Lithuania where there were also pogroms?

But then I discovered my grandfather's obituary which reveals that my grandfather was in fact born in Middlesbrough, England in 1899 so that totally undermines my theories and what I thought I'd always been told. He was born in Yorkshire so clearly, he didn't travel from Russia at all. Then I wondered if in fact the rest of the family had left during earlier pogroms in the 1890s but the facts reveal that that's not correct either.

On reading my aunt's notes about her life (which are very brief about her parents' background) I see that she understood that my grandfather was the youngest of the five children of a *second* marriage with a wealthy woman from the Jewish community called Jane Solomon. Indeed, he seems to have had a son by that previous marriage. The photograph below shows the family. I also have a version of the same photograph annotated with my aunt's writing. Going from left to right it shows Horace 1894, *"Aaron – stepbrother? Born 1884?"* (standing at the back), Judith (no date), Bernard 1897, Cyril 1891, and sitting on the ground at the front, the youngest, my grandfather, Frank 1899. I've now done more research and although my aunt was right that there was another brother, he was not called Aaron nor was he a stepbrother. My grandfather's other brother was in fact his half brother and was the one who was called Isaac.

The Benjamins: Horace, Jane, Isaac, Judith, Bernard, Hyman, Cyril and my grandfather, Frank, in sailor outfit on the ground

So, in my imagination, my grandfather left Russia as a small boy with his family at the time of the Odessa pogrom and made the journey to England from Russia, but from this it looks as if it must have been his father and step brother who had that experience. In fact, even that turns out not to be correct as researching the story of Hyman's first wife makes clear.

The Cemetery Scribes make it clear that my great-grandfather, Hyman Benjamin, got married a second time to Jane Solomon of Bushey, Hertfordshire, this time in 1889 in Paddington. And by 1891 she's recorded as living with him at The Avenue, Linthorpe, Middlesbrough in the same year that the eldest of her five children was born, Horace. Who knows why Hyman met a woman from Bushey and got married in Paddington? I have no idea. But we do know that she was his second wife.

Once you have a name, a great deal emerges from the internet (many thanks here to my brother, Mark, who looked this up) so the name Jane Solomon has been very helpful. Whilst all the family trees which others have tried to put together show my great-grandfather as Isaac Benjamin, he was in fact called Hyman Benjamin. There are several references which make this clear. The Royal College of Physicians published an obituary of my grandfather in which the opening lines read, *"Francis Joseph Bentley was born at Middlesbrough, Yorkshire, the son of Hyman Benjamin and his wife Jane Solomon."*

So who was the first wife, the mother of Isaac, the stepbrother? The Cemetery Scribes refer to Hyman Benjamin, born in 1854 in Russia/Poland, married first to Rachel Tuchman in 1876 in Sheffield. They had two sons, one who died as a baby in 1877 and the second, Isaac, born in 1883. So this means it was her surviving son, Isaac, who was the stepbrother in the family photograph and not someone called Aaron.

Rachel died in 1887 at the age of 32 and was buried in Middlesbrough Old Jewish Cemetery. The inscription on her tomb reads, *"Sacred to the memory of Rachel the beloved wife of Hyman Benjamin and affectionate daughter of Rev. J. Tuchman"* (Cemetery Scribes).The notes also state that the Hebrew inscription records she was *"Rachel bat (?) Rabbi of the Holy Congregation of Portsmouth."* At that time, rabbis did use the title "Rev." so this may not be an error in translation but indicate that her father was indeed a rabbi. But whether she was Jewish or not, this shows that she and Hyman got married in 1876 in Sheffield. So this totally undermines the idea that Hyman left Russia with either wife or any children.

Hyman clearly moved to England at least some time before his marriage to Rachel in Sheffield in 1876. So he may have been an economic migrant rather than someone who escaped the pogroms, although there were pogroms throughout the 19th century. No doubt he was escaping both persecution and poverty. But it seems clear that he did this as a young man and not with either his first or his second family. I assume that the families will have grown up knowing the true story. But maybe they didn't talk about it or maybe they didn't pass on the truth. Maybe this was another of the silences.

Below is the Benjamin family tree. No doubt there are other children who I don't know about but this version does seem to be accurate.

The story of the Middlesbrough Jewish community is interesting. Hyman was an early arrival so the background is important context.

In 1801, Middlesbrough consisted of no more than a single farm house. In 1828 the influential Quaker banker, coal mine owner and Stockton and Darlington Railways shareholder, Joseph Pease sailed up the River Tees to find a suitable new site downriver of Stockton on which to place new coal staithes. In 1829 he and a group of Quaker bought the Middlesbrough farmstead and associated estate, and established the Middlesbrough Estate Company.

With the advent of the Industrial Revolution, iron and coal and the proximity to the sea, it soon grew and became famous for its steel works and shipbuilding; an industrial powerhouse also became a busy centre for imported goods from the continent. For many Jews who emigrated, their first sight of England will have been the River Tees. It's helpful to imagine the scene. Wikipedia reveals that in 1846 one local writer observed: "To the stranger visiting his home after an absence of fifteen years, this proud array of ships, docks, warehouses, churches, foundries and wharfs would seem like some enchanted spectacle, some Arabian Night's vision."

The first Jew to settle in Middlesbrough was one Maurice Levy in 1862. A report in the *Middlesbrough Weekly News and Cleveland Advertiser* of 5th October 1865 stated

"Arrangements have just been completed and premises secured in Lower East Street for the holding of worship according to the Mosaic Ritual. The advent of a larger number of Jews into the town has called for the opening of this new place of Worship" (The Jewish JCR-UK).

The Benjamin Family

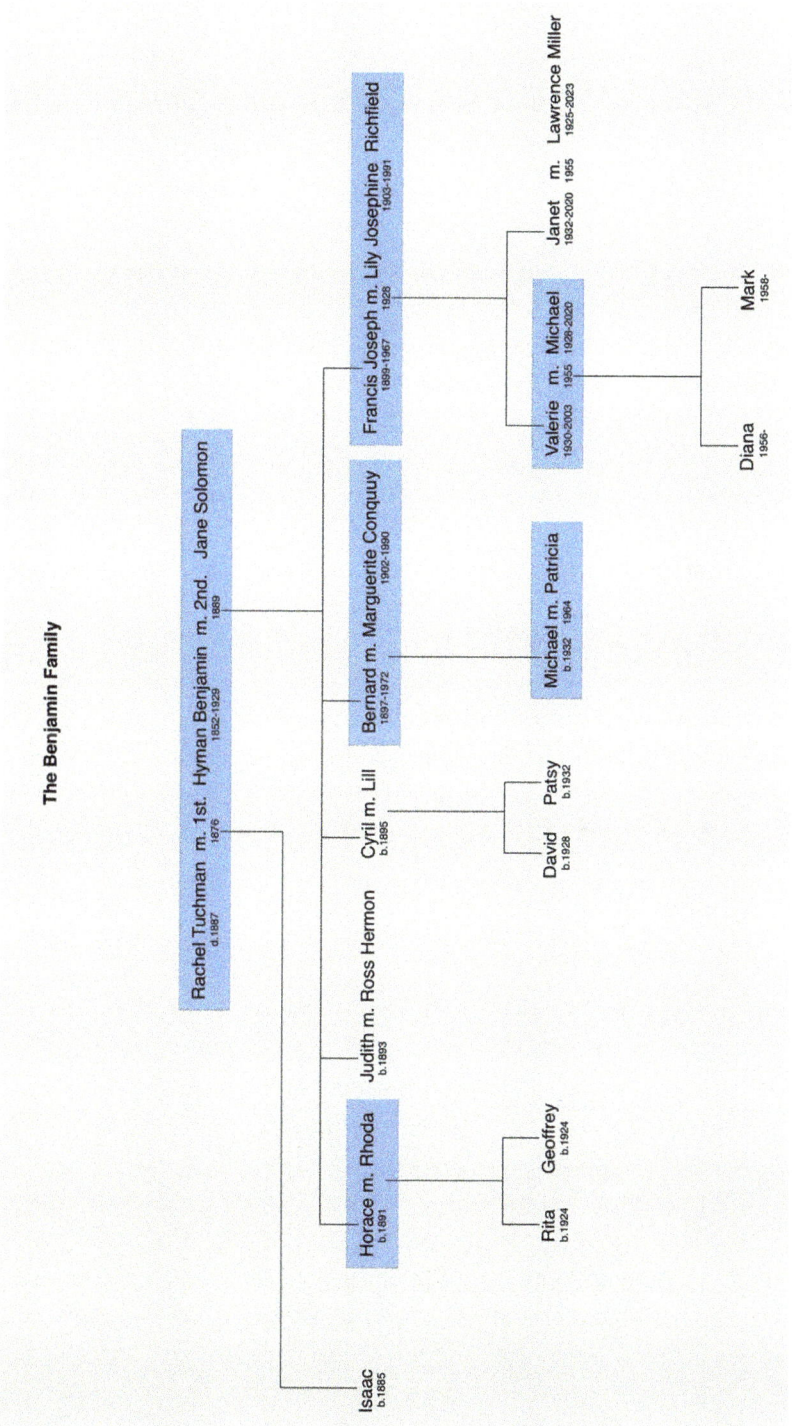

The *Newcastle Chronicle* of 26th May 1870 stated: "On Saturday a synagogue was opened at Hill Street, Middlesbrough. About seven years ago (1863) Mr Levy and his family came to live at Middlesbrough and shortly after that Mr I Alston went to reside in that town". A few weeks later more Jewish families from Poland and Russia came to Middlesbrough and they worshipped in the house of Messrs. Levy and his son-in-law Alston" (Extract from *The Jewish Communities of North East England* by Lewis Olsover, published by Ashley Mark Publishing Co, 1980).

A descendant of Alston, "Mr. B. H. Alston, then of Melbourne, Australia, wrote to ... in 1935. Recalling his childhood days in Middlesbrough, he stated, "Gradually as the first Jews began to arrive in Middlesbrough, either from Poland or Russia, we were able to form a Minyan, the services being held either at my Grandfather or Father's home. Each of these gentlemen possessed a Sefer Torah. My Grandfather brought his from Poland. A year or two later, my Father engaged rooms which were fitted up in two divisions for males and females. One of these rooms was no more than a loft over a Joiner's shop. 1 was the first boy Barmitzvah in this temporary Synagogue in 1872 before the present Synagogue was built" (The Jewish JCR-UK).

The Jewish population of Middlesbrough grew as more immigrants arrived, the new synagogue was opened in June 1874, and land was acquired for a Jewish cemetery in the 1880s. Before the building of the Transporter Bridge in 1911, burial was very difficult because the nearest cemetery was the other side of the River Tees and the journey was a long one so the acquisition of the land for the cemetery made a great difference and shows how much the community had grown. It was only much later in the 1960s that the population dwindled and in 1998 the synagogue had to close.

But when Hyman Benjamin arrived he was one of the early Jewish arrivals in this industrial boom town and the Ashkenazi congregation was growing. Hyman clearly became an important figure in this community. "Hyman Benjamin" is listed in the Jewish JCR-UK as having been president of the lay officers of the congregation three times: 1898-1901, 1904-1907, and

1916-1917. And one "H. Benjamin" is listed as having been president between 1947 and 1948, and also treasurer on several occasions. This may well have been Hyman's son, Horace.

The Kehilat Middlesbrough Newsletter and Archives contains these fascinating notes by one Sam Smith, 1957, about the man who was my great-grandfather. It would definitely seem to be him as it refers to him having had two wives, the second Jane Solomon, and having had several children by her, including Horace. It's a very glowing piece and perhaps goes over the top but either way he was obviously a significant figure.

"Hyman Benjamin (1852-1929)

The most popular and endearing member of the Congregation was Hyman Benjamin. He was an outstanding personality. A most likeable man. Kind, considerate and approachable; religious and strictly orthodox with the interest of the Synagogue and Congregation always at heart. To charity he never turned a deaf ear.

He was many times President and so highly esteemed and respected was on two occasions presented with an Illuminated Address for his work and interest in the Community.

He was twice married. By his first wife Rachel (nee Tuchman) he had two children. One died in infancy. The other was the late Ike Benjamin, and by his second had several children, one the late Horace Benjamin.

He was all an ideal Jew should be; fair, just, sympathetic and conscientious and this he was in business and all transactions.

In business he was a moneylender with offices in Albert Road, and invested largely in cottage property, in which respect he was one of the biggest owners in the town and not one of his many tenants could reprove him for inconsiderateness, unfairness, or harshness. He lent a willing and compassionate ear to all complaints which he never failed to rectify and is remembered and esteemed to this day, leaving an untarnished name, a synonym for probity and a credit to Jewry. He relished a joke, or humorous story as no other and extracted every drop of vintage from them which often threw him into paroxysms of laughter.

He had charm of manner, was pleasant and amiable, indeed one of Nature's gentlemen. He was always well groomed and carefully dressed, for he took a great pride in his personal appearance, which was that of a prosperous city magnate.

He resided at 5 The Avenue Linthorpe with his second wife Jane, and after her death, which left him almost prostrate, he lived with his son Horace at "Westhoe" in Eastbourne Rd where he died, greatly mourned and beloved by both Jew and Gentile".

So this paints a very clear picture of a highly respected and successful family who brought their sons up to be professionals. Here is a photograph of the proud parents and their son, Francis, my grandfather at the age of 18 and therefore a new medical student at Durham University. From left to right they are Jane Solomon, Hyman Benjamin, and Francis Benjamin.

Jane, Hyman, and Frank Benjamin

I know nothing about the Benjamin family from my grandparents as neither they nor my mother ever spoke about them. The more I piece the history together the more it becomes apparent that there was a significant rupture. I know that Hyman supported my grandfather through Durham University to become a doctor and that Grandpa had a distinguished career. They seem to have been quite a close family and certainly Grandpa and Bernard were close enough to go down to London together and plan on marrying the two sisters, Jo and Marguerite.

I know that the name Benjamin became Bentley, a good Yorkshire name. I'd always thought the whole family had done it on arrival in England but that's obviously wrong. My mother's birth certificate makes it clear that she was born Valerie Bentley so they'd clearly changed their name by then. The dates reveal that my grandparents married in 1928, my great grandfather died the following year, and not long after that they changed their name. I knew them both as atheists who had rejected Judaism shortly after their marriage.

I suspect that the wealthy, influential and orthodox Hyman Benjamin did not approve of my grandmother who had not been brought up Jewish and was a shop model. And, of course, the planned double wedding (which I now understand is frowned on in Judaism as risking bad luck) did indeed end in tragedy. At some point, there must have been a terrible rift which resulted in the silence and the huge gaps in my knowledge.

This next photograph is revealing. It comes from an album of Granny's which I'd not seen before. It shows her writing beneath the picture, saying that it was taken in June 1928. She, Jo, is sitting next to Grandpa's parents, Jane and Hyman Benjamin. She is smiling broadly to camera with dark glasses on. There are two men standing behind the parents but neither of them are my grandfather, Frank. It's not a formal studio photo and no one has straightened their clothes, which look crumpled out, so it looks as if it must have been taken at home by my grandfather. Hyman is not looking comfortable at all. I think the two young men behind must be Cyril and Horace, two of Frank's older brothers. On the basis that the photograph was taken in June 1928 (so my grandmother's handwriting indicates) it must have been taken not all that long after their wedding. Given the circumstances of the wedding, Granny had probably barely met her parents-in-law. They certainly came from totally different backgrounds; the Benjamins established and wealthy and part of the thriving Jewish community in Middlesbrough, with their educated and professional sons, and Granny the good-time girl and shop model from Carnaby Street, Hungarian, and not brought up Jewish. I don't get the sense of great family joy from this photograph.

Jane is looking fondly at her son taking the photograph but Hyman is looking distinctly uncomfortable. Everyone seems to have sat down quite fast as if to get it over with. But Granny is smiling broadly in her dark glasses. Within a year Hyman Benjamin was dead, the older brother, Horace, took over the business, my grandparents changed their name to Bentley and rejected Judaism. It must have been a significant rift.

My grandmother, Jo, seated on the right with her in-laws, 1928

Two recent discoveries reveal the extent of what seems to have been the ensuing family rupture.

Through my cousin Tim's family tree work, I discover that my grandfather's eldest brother, Horace, and his wife, Rhoda, had twins (Rita and Geoffrey, born in 1924). When I had twins and was surprised that there were none in the family, my mother told me that there may have been a great-great Russian uncle who had had twins. What she did not say is that she had cousins who were twins and putting different memories together, I believe that she knew them.

She and her sister, Janet, were evacuated out of London during the war to stay with their Aunt Rhoda. I recall Mummy telling me that Rhoda hadn't been at all nice to them. I remember the name because it's a name I wasn't familiar with. She was Horace's wife. If there had been a big family rift after the marriage, a change of name and rejection of Judaism, it must have been difficult for them to have Valerie and Janet to stay. Since the twins were then teenagers they were probably not very interested in their unknown and much younger cousins. But it must have been more than an age difference that caused the coldness for Mummy never to have told me about them. I suspect it would have stirred up bad memories that were best left alone. Janet's notes say that when my grandparents changed their name there was no ill feeling with his "strict Jewish family" but I don't think that can be right. Certainly there was some ongoing relationship with Grandpa's brother, Bernard, but that seemed cool and I never heard of any other relations and all the indications are of a significant split.

The pattern of lost cousins was repeated some 80 years later. In 2021, I received an email out of the blue from a probate lawyer representing the estate of someone called Patricia Benjamin who had left money in her will to her husband Michael's long lost cousins who included my mother and aunt. The lawyer had used genealogists to track me down. As a result of this contact, I heard from another distant cousin, Tony Salem, who knew more about the background. He told me that Patricia's husband, Michael Benjamin, was the son of Bernard, my grandfather's brother who was due to have married Granny's favourite sister, Marguerite, before she died just before the wedding. Bernard had subsequently married another woman called Marguerite Conquy. I do remember meeting Bernard and Marguerite but Granny was never very keen on the new Marguerite so it was all a bit frosty. And indeed one of my father's letters to Mary Chait (when he was trying to find out more) refers to Mummy having been rather "cool" about Bernard and Marguerite.

What I learned from Tony Salem was that when Bernard and Marguerite's son, Michael, married Patricia, she said that she wanted him to have no contact with his Jewish family. This resulted in another family rupture and explains yet more silence since one of the family he was not to have contact with was my mother and her family. Patricia died without children. So her will leaves legacies to a variety of others. She left £2,000 to her Burmese cats and the vets who were charged with looking after them and £5,000 to some named individuals. The will divided the balance between a list of charities and her husband's long lost cousins. I wonder why she left anything to the cousins who she had prevented her husband from contacting? Perhaps she felt guilty. Perhaps she had no idea that my grandparents had rejected Judaism and had brought their daughters up in an atheist home. We (the lost cousins and their children, totalling nine people including me, my brother and my two cousins), turned out to be the lucky ones because with the increase in house values, each received £25,000 out of the blue from someone I'd never heard of. And it also opened a door for me with a glimpse of more information about the family.

How complicated families are. When I went on a *Guardian* masterclass course about how to write a family history, the tutor told us that one of the problems with writing about family is where to start and where to stop as it is all part of human life and there is no beginning and no end to any of our family histories. I think of my family as a very small one. I had two aunts and have only two cousins. Alex had two aunts and has four cousins. But, of course, there are many extended family members out there. We just don't know about them.

What Tony Salem opened up for me is a bit about the second Marguerite, Marguerite Conquy, the one who wasn't Granny's beloved older sister. He told me that Marguerite's father, Solomon Conquy, was a rabbi from Gibraltar and her mother was French (Henriette Diefenthal). Tony's father has the Salem family tree which stretches back to 1700. This shows that his great grandfather was Dutch and his wife was from Birmingham. And there are many descendants. This is just one example of how big a "family" really is. But that part of the jigsaw is not my story so I will leave it there.

4. Hungary: The Reichenfelds and the Ronas

What I knew from my Hungarian grandmother, Jo Bentley, is that her maiden name was Josephine Richfield (originally Reichenfeld) and that her mother (Lina) had become Jewish so as to marry her father (Miksa or Max). The family moved from Hungary to London but soon after that he left home. So her mother had had to bring up their five children by herself.

I now know more than I did thanks to the memories recorded and research done by Mary Chait, the daughter of Granny's cousin, Laci, who I've had the great good fortune to talk to. She writes,

"Miksa (Max) had got his cook into trouble – she insisted on marriage (apparently with a carving knife) and converted to Judaism. Miksa and Lina (nee Szenszel) called their first daughter Rosie. She was born in Hungary, followed by Tibor. Max's grandchildren are not in agreement about the place of birth of Marguerite, the next child. Janet thinks she too was born in Hungary, but Valerie and Dennis think she was born in Britain. Josephine, two years younger than Marguerite, was born in Britain in 1903, followed by Alfred in 1905. Only Rosalie could speak Hungarian. Lina opened a restaurant in Foubert Place, off Carnaby St., mainly serving lunches to office workers. She was assisted by Bona, her widowed sister, and the family lived upstairs. At some point Max disappeared to Germany, but it's not quite clear to me exactly when, or whether he had any contact with Lina and the children afterwards".

One of the really strange things which I can't work out is that my grandmother was clear that she and her sister, Marguerite, were only told that they were in fact Jewish after their mother told them that they were wasting their time with Frank and Bernard and yet both the 1911 census and a family photograph show that this can't be correct. There is also a photograph of the family

Photograph of Lina Reichenfeld, Granny's mother

which clearly shows her father in the midst of the family many years later. First, I've found the London census of 1911 filled out in Max's handwriting (which matches his signature) showing all seven of the Reichenfield family living at 26 Foubert Place. It states that the children were aged between 13 and 7, that he was running a restaurant, that the first three were born in Hungary and that my grandmother was born in Bristol and the youngest, Alfred, in London. This suggests that they moved to England between 1901 and 1903 and first went to Bristol before settling in London. The census also makes clear that it was crowded living, with seven of them in two tenement rooms just round the corner from Carnaby Street.

Here's the photo below which has Granny's writing on the back giving the ages of the children as 15 (the eldest, Rosalie), Tibor, 13, Marguerite, 11, Josephine (Granny) aged 9, the youngest Alfred, aged 7, and the father very definitely sitting in the middle of the family group. What I'd always understood (and the notes made by my Aunt Janet also confirm) is that their father, Max, left home shortly after Alfred was born. Did he come home after some years? Did he not explain that he was Jewish? Did he reject his Judaism on arrival in England?

The Reichenfelds: Tibor, Lina, max, Josephine, Rosalie, Alfred and Marguerite

Mary Chait also has a copy of this photo and in her own family history also says how mystified she is by the mismatch between what she'd also grown up understanding about Miksa's leaving the family and the visual evidence. Mary writes that Miksa left for Germany and spent the First World War there where he perhaps had to hide the fact that he was Jewish. She also says that Rosalie, the eldest daughter, was registered as an enemy alien and had to report regularly to the police station. But that still leaves a lot of questions begged. A mystery. Well, to be honest, I prefer the version of the story we all grew up being told in which the telegram was sent up to Yorkshire revealing that Josephine and

Marguerite were in fact Jewish. And, as is the way, with family stories, this is the one which sticks.

Who did I know in this Hungarian family? I knew the eldest Rosalie (or Rosa) who lived in St John's Wood and who I learn was named after her grandmother (as were so many of the family) and was born in Hungary. I also met the youngest, Alfred, who lived outside Brighton. Tibor had left the family at some point like his father and was never mentioned and poor Marguerite died a tragic death.

Of the rest of the family and Granny's nine cousins, the only one I was aware of Granny keeping in touch with and who I knew was Laci Rona (pronounced Lotzi). Laci was Granny's father's nephew, the son of Miksa's younger brother, Simon. Laci Rona was a lovely man. I liked him very much. He and his wife, Judy, came to our wedding. He was fun and kind and knew how to make small children laugh. But he'd experienced terrible sadness and extraordinary times. Judy survived Auschwitz unlike nearly everyone else in their two families. They married and had children but in 1956 they had to escape over the border when the Russian tanks rolled in to suppress the Hungarian Uprising. I'll come to those extraordinary times later as there are moving records of what happened. But first I'll cover what I know about the background to the whole Reichenfeld Hungarian family thanks to the fantastic research done by Mary Chait (Laci and Judy's daughter) into our shared family, starting with our mutual great-grandfather.

The Reichenfeld family in the 19th and early 20th century

What the Hungarian family tree shows is that the Reichenfelds were, or used to be, extensive. Granny's father (Miksa or Max) and Laci's father (Simon) had five other siblings (NB: All but Hermine went on to have children but I only have room for those I'm going to write about and I've highlighted those who will be the focus in the text below to help identify them).

My great-great-grandfather was Adolf Reichenfeld, born in 1845 (the name Adolf was a popular name in Austro-Hungary although with terrible connotations today). Their mother was Rozalia Grosz, born in 1846. Adolf's father was Jozsef (also referred to as Juda) Reichenfeld. He was born in 1822 and is referred to in the records as a "pedlar". His wife was called Jozefa Heimler. Mary's research indicates that the name Heimler was a well-known name in North West Hungary, and that the many Heimlers were related and had moved first to Bavaria from Spain, which mean that they were Sephardic Jews, although my DNA reveals only Ashkenazi Jewish background.

Adolf and Rozalia Reichenfeld had seven children: Jani (Jack), Lina, Wolf (known as Vili or Willy), Miksa, Janka, Simon (born 23rd January 1878), and Hermine. Rozalia died at the age of 42 when Simon (Laci's father) was only 10. As Mary says, *"Rozalia's children must have missed her very much and kept her memory alive – five of them named a daughter after her"* (including of course my great-aunt Rosalie).

Mary has clear family records with names and dates. She explains that it is thanks to the right wing government in Hungary in the 1930s (who were always suspicious of Jews) that there are such carefully kept central records of the Jewish population, which she has been able to search. Her father had had to produce birth certificates of previous generations in order to prove that they were Hungarian and she still has these.

I learned from Mary that Adolf and Rozalia had a double wedding on 23rd December 1867, together with her sister, Roza Grosz and his cousin, Moritz Reichenfeld. Mary says that, *"It came as a complete surprise to me when I saw the actual entries in the register that this was in fact a double wedding. For one thing, double weddings are discouraged, if not forbidden, by Jewish tradition, and for another there was of course no clue from the marriage certificate in my possession, nor do I remember Apu (her father) ever mentioning it"*. That's fascinating because history repeated itself with Adolf's grandchild (my grandmother), Jo, having planned her tragically ill-fated double wedding 60 years later. It's also interesting to learn that Laci never mentioned this double wedding to his daughter as the tragic coincidence would have been well known to him since he was close to my grandmother

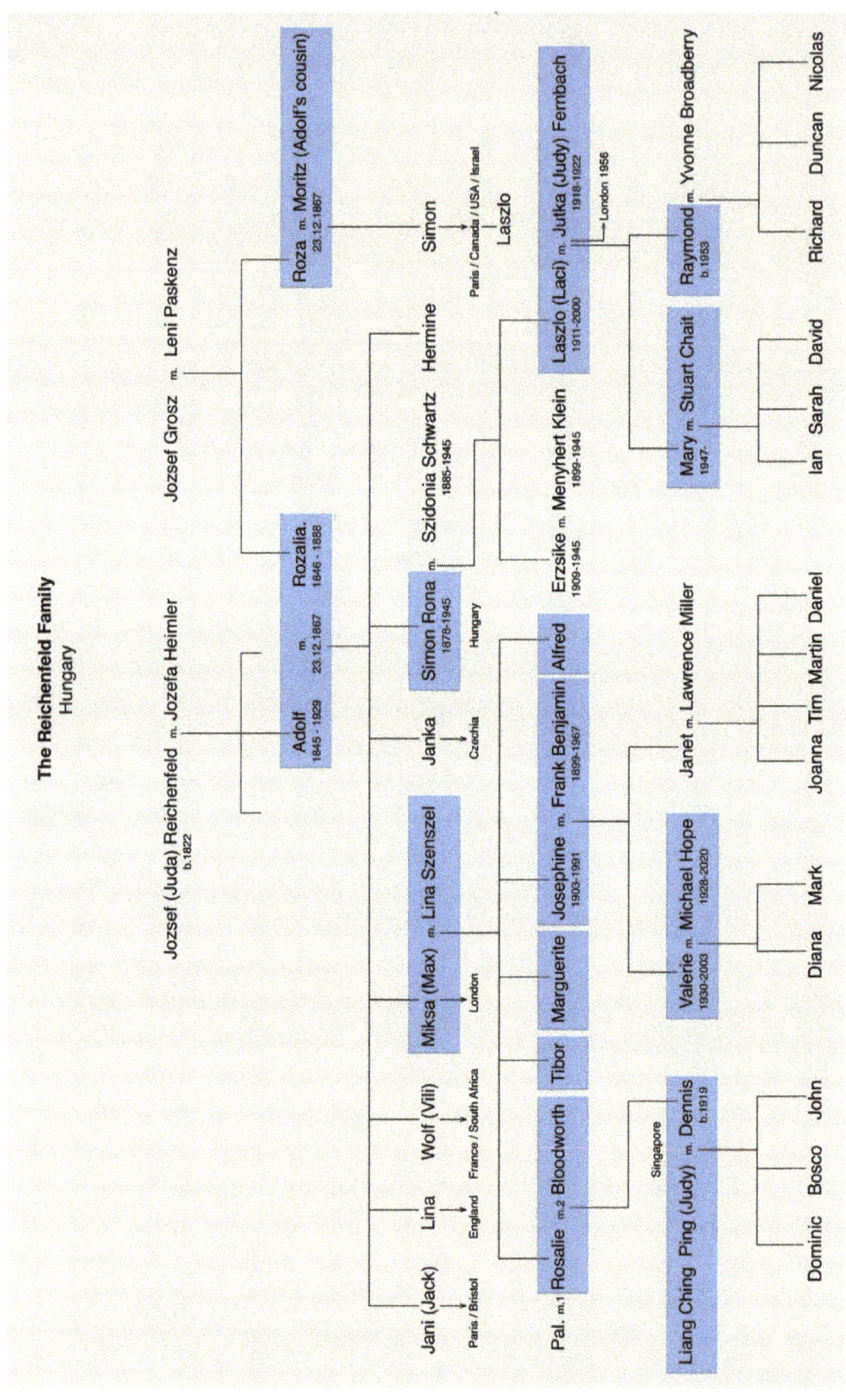

and would have known about Marguerite's death just before their double wedding. Another family silence. There are many things which it is too painful to discuss.

Where did the Reichenfelds live? The extensive family of Reichenfelds all lived in North West Hungary in villages near Gyor, a pretty-looking town with typical Austro-Hungarian architecture, close to the Slovakian border. Adolf and Rozalia and family lived in a village called Gyorasszonfya, a pretty place as the picture in the postcard below shows. Mary explains that she has found 248 Reichenfelds in the area and believes that the whole family must have adopted the German name as far back as the 1780s when surnames became compulsory throughout the Hapsburg Empire.

Postcard of Gyorasszonfya, Hungary where the Reichenfeld family came from

Mary visited Hungary both with her father after her mother's death and again after her father's death in order to see the places where the Reichenfelds had lived. She writes, "*We visited Hungary in August 2002 by car and had the chance to explore the places mentioned in the records, so that they are no longer just names to me. Following the advice of a Jewish lady who still lives in Gyor, we sought out the mayor's office in Gyorasszonyfa, where our Reichenfelds lived in the first half of the nineteenth century, and where they might well have taken up the surname. The building housing the office was erected in 1848 and therefore part of the village where our ancestors lived, together with the church, which was built in 1793. The mayor was very pleased to see us and knew the name Reichenfeld straightaway. He spent a great deal of time with us, telling us about the history of the village and the Jewish community which existed there from the beginning of the eighteenth century until the summer of 1944, when the Jews still living in the village were deported to Auschwitz by the Nazi occupiers. He took us to see the joint memorial the village has erected to the murdered Jews and the members of the village who lost their lives on the battlefield, listing in alphabetical order the names of all those who died. He also showed us where the synagogue and Jewish school had once been".* In 1851 a third of the village population of 810 were Jewish. In 1944 there were only a dozen who were soon deported to their deaths. *"One of the present day Jewish inhabitants of Gyor is a music teacher who was pleased to show us round and tell us something of its history. There were 5000 Jews there in 1944, of whom ninety percent perished in the camps – most of the rest have left since. However, those who live there now have an organised community and the synagogue has been restored".*

"Many of the entries record the occupation of the person who has died, the bridegroom, or the father of the bridegroom or the newborn baby. Like Adolf Reichenfeld, his father and father-in-law, many were pedlars, while others were tailors or inn-keepers. On the occasion of our visit to Gyorasszonyfa, I asked the mayor what being a pedlar would have meant. He told me that Adolf and the others would have gone round the farms looking for merchandise that would be marketable, such as feathers to be made into pens, and leather. They would then take the goods they had selected to bigger towns and cities where they sold them to manufacturers. Today we don't think of pedlars as very well-off people, but apparently many of these were prosperous."

The Family Diaspora

All of Adolf and Rozalia's seven children (except Simon) left Hungary in a diaspora which spread to London, Paris, the USA, and what is now the Czech Republic. Simon, the sixth child, was the only one of the seven children to stay in Hungary and he, his wife and daughter all died in the Holocaust.

In contrast to Russia, there were no pogroms driving Jews out of Hungary in the 19th and early 20th centuries and it remained a relatively safe place for Jews up until the end of the war. Although some did well before the war, for others it was often economic necessity which drove them to leave. In the case of the Reichenfelds, the eldest Jani (or Jack), a tailor, wanted to leave after the death of his mother and his father's remarriage. He moved first to Paris and subsequently to Bristol. From the London census of 1911 it is clear that when Max and Lina Reichenfeld (my great-grandparents) moved to England, they first followed Jack to Bristol where my grandmother was born, and only after that moved to London. Vili also first moved to France but then to England and some of his family subsequently to South Africa. The other siblings also moved to England although Lina then moved on to America. Janka married and settled in what is now the Czech Republic and was able to leave with her family around 1938. Meanwhile the descendants of Roza and Moritz (of the double wedding with Adolf and Rozalia) moved to Paris (many of whom Mary knows to be alive today) and onwards to America, Canada, and Israel.

When trying to research and write about the history of the family it soon becomes apparent that names, both first and surname, are confusing. Even with records it's not that easy to track down individuals because of the endless changing of names. First the surnames had changed from whatever was the original Jewish name to Reichenfeld probably as long as ago as the late 18th century. The Austro-Hungarian empire's ruling language was German until 1848 so a German name was a wise name to adopt and as we can see all the older generation had German surnames. I've also wondered about the choice of the name Reichenfeld as it could mean both the king's land as well as a rich field. Given this double meaning it was an interesting choice as in medieval times (certainly in England) Jews were known as being both the king's property and also under his protection, an interesting combination of ideas.

After family members moved to England they adopted an English name "Richfield". Meanwhile, still in Hungary, Simon Reichenfeld changed his name to Rona, a Hungarian name. This explains what always mystified me, which is why Granny's closest cousin, Laci Rona, had a different surname to the rest of the family.

First names are also confusing not only because names were frequently repeated both across and down through generations (see the number of times the name Rozalia was used in various versions) but different names were adopted on immigration to another country so many were known by several names. So Miksa became Max, and Jutka became Judy, but she was also known as both Juliana and Judith.

"What's in a name?" Shakespeare uses this line in *Romeo and Juliet* to indicate that the name itself is irrelevant but in this history of Jewish immigration the name is far from irrelevant. When I spoke to Mary I asked her what I should call her. She laughed and said, 'My name is the story of my life'. She was born "Maria" in 1947, not a Jewish name and presumably chosen deliberately. On arrival in England she became known as Mary. Then her Jewish adopted name became Miriam but many of her official records still name her as Maria or Mary. So she goes by all three names and in public records it can be very confusing. Her brother was born Gabor, was renamed Gabriel on arrival in England, but later chose to change his name to Raymond.

In the confusing business of changing and similar names, it's interesting to note that while most of the Reichenfelds moved to London (except for Simon), the other half of the 1867 double wedding (Rozalia's sister, Roza, and Moritz, Adolf's cousin) also named one of their sons Simon (born only a few months later than Simon Rona in 1878). Not only that but one of their grandchildren was also called Laszlo (or Laci) and was born in the same year (1911) as his double cousin, our Laci Rona. As Mary says, *"This means Apu (Daddy) had a second cousin with the same name, the same year of birth, a father with the same name born in the same year, and a grandmother with almost the identical first name and surname"*.

I haven't done the research that Mary has done but when I put the name Reichenfeld into the internet it's extraordinary that what comes up immediately is the name Simon Reichenfeld. In fact, two Simon Reichenfelds come up, both born in 1878, one in a place called Nyalka to a mother, Roza, and a father, Moric, and a second born in Gyor to a mother, Roza, and a father, Moric, and then a third also born in Nyalka but in 1887. All three died in 1945 in Poland. There were either many Simon Reichenfelds or the genealogy websites have the wrong information, but either way they all suffered the same cruel death.

The Ronas: Hungary

It's important to me to talk about the Rona family, Granny's Hungarian cousins, who were the family who stayed in Hungary at the beginning of the 20th century and who changed their name from Reichenfeld to Rona. Laci and Judy Rona were close to my grandparents. They were good friends and were the only family members who I recall my grandparents cherishing. In fact, if I look at the family tree, the only people I ever heard of or met (other than Granny's sister, Rosalie, and brother, Alfred, and once briefly Grandpa's brother, Bernard) were Laci and Judy Rona. I now know that Granny's sisters, Rosalie and Marguerite, visited the Rona family in the early 1920s and my grandparents went to visit in the 1930s. So the Rona family mattered to them then and later even more so.

Here's a letter from Laci to my cousin, Tim, written in 1996 when he was 85. I can hear his voice and his soft Hungarian accent as I read his handwriting and it warms my heart.

"Dear Tim. 27.3.96

I am very pleased to hear about you. We have a very deep root between the Bentley and Rona family! I have heard of you by Raymond and of course by your parents. When will you come to London. I hope we can meet together. First I met with your family in 1931 when Frank and Josephine your grandparents have spent a few days in Budapest. We have not had a common language, even so we were able to build up an excellent relation between us. The world war prevented to meet again. Jan 1956 your granma Josephine sent to me a telegram writing me to escape to the UK. With great difficulties we did cross the Hungarian/Austrian border. When we arrived to London your granma have made a tremendous effort to help me and contributed to settle down.

I appreciate very much that you want to know the origin of our family and to make a family tree. I enclose herewith my graph and you have to forgive me for the mistakes for I am sure I did.

Hope that we shall meet sometime in the near future. I send my love to you.

Laci"

Mary describes meeting me for the first time after they left Budapest and moved to London. "*Jo Bentley, who had sent us the telegram at the time of the uprising, took it upon herself to organise financial help for us from all the family to tide us over till we got on our feet. When we visited Jo and Frank in Brentwood, where Frank was an eminent doctor, both their daughters Valerie and Janet were pregnant – Janet was expecting her first baby, but Valerie already had a little girl, Diana. Jo and Frank were both keen painters and must have had one of the first cameras capable of colour photography: a photo taken at Brentwood in 1957 of Diana, Raymond and me is the first colour photograph in our family album*".

Mary's notes say that this photo was taken in 1957 but Mummy wasn't pregnant with Mark until 1958 (he was born in October 1958) so I think this photo was taken when I was two. In that case it was taken when we'd already left Germany and Daddy was posted to the USA for 6 months leaving Mummy and me

Letter from Laci Rona to my cousin, Timothy Miller

At my grandparents: me, Mary and Gabriel Rona in 1958

living with both Grannies, first in Brentwood (in this photo) and then in Lancashire until he came back and they found a house in Bolton. This peripatetic period was not a happy time, as I have since discovered, but that's another story to be told another time.

The war was very cruel to the Rona family. Laci was in a forced labour camp, Judy was in Auschwitz and both lost nearly all of their families. Then, in 1956, they had to flee over the border when the Russian tanks rolled in. (They were among the 200,000 Hungarian refugees who fled). Their daughter, Mary, has some extraordinary documentation both about the liberation in 1945 and the long journey Judy made back from the camp as well as the Rona family's escape over the border from the Russian tanks in 1956.

I had no idea that there were such extensive and important records of these terrible times. I see from the papers which were in my father's trunk of family papers that my mother had been in touch with Mary in 2001 (in fact, there are fairly frequent emails) and been sent Mary's notes including the journal of Judy's forced march from the camp but she never mentioned this to me and I wonder if she told my father as he also wrote to Mary in 2013, seemingly in ignorance of the earlier correspondence and was sent similar material. It may well have been too hard to take in and not been something she wanted to talk about. And, of course, by 2002, Mummy was not well. Her brain tumour was diagnosed only seven weeks before she died on 19 May 2003 so this may also be an explanation for why I'm only now discovering all of this.

I feel very affected by the documents I've now read because although the persecution and escape as refugees is not the story of my family, it could well have been if Hitler had managed to invade England. My grandparents and my mother were very alive to how close this was and I remember them talking about how fortunate they were. The Ronas were close family so to read about family members who I knew as a child having survived Auschwitz and escaped over the border from Russian tanks in 1956, the year I was born, is particularly important to me. It has always shaped my sense of who I am and what I care about.

I'm incredibly grateful to Mary for her family history and for the records she has of Judy's liberation after Auschwitz and their escape from the Russians in 1956. I've wrestled with whether or not to include all the detail here as it makes extraordinary, if tough, reading. But I realise that this is the story of the Rona family and not mine, however affected I have been by it. So I'm going to describe it here but leave the verbatim records in the Appendices at the end so that anyone who wants to can read the full original documents.

The Ronas 1939 to 1945

Before the war, both Laci and his wife-to-be, Judy Fernbach, lived in the Budapest area. Until the German occupation in 1944, Hungary was a relatively safe haven, even during the war, so many Jewish refugees had moved there from other countries. But it was only relative.

Even before the German occupation, the Horthy regime and its anti-Jewish regulations were closing in on everyone. Jews were not allowed to go to university and many were denied the right to be employed. Both Laci and Judy lost their jobs; in Laci's case his employers received a letter from the authorities requiring them to sack Laci who was referred to by name. Jews were also not allowed to join the army but were put into forced labour camps where many others did not survive. The first time Laci was called up he paid to have his appendix removed so that he was declared not fit for work. The surgeon did this to help people but he was later caught and everyone involved had to be interrogated. Laci was lucky to be interviewed by a well-known liberal who let him go after shouting at him for the benefit of those listening. The next time he was called up he had to go. It was very hard. On one occasion, half of the unit were marched off and never came back.

And there were killings. From the German invasion of Russia in 1941 Hungary took on the status of Germany's ally. Peter Hidas, in his outline of the history of Hungarian Jews, states that 18,000 Jews who could not prove their Hungarian citizenship were deported to Galicia in 1941 and shot by the SS and their henchmen. Judy thought that two of her Fernbach uncles were among them, Vilmos and Izidor.

Then in March 1944, Germany occupied Hungary and German tanks rolled into Budapest. Adolf Eichmann was sent to supervise:

yellow star and ghettoization laws were put in place within eight weeks, families had their homes confiscated. Jews were forced to move into designated houses and the Jews in the provinces were systematically deported to Auschwitz. Jews in the outskirts of Budapest were the last to be taken before the deportations were stopped in July 1944. Both Laci's parents and Judy and her family were in this group. Vast numbers of people were deported to the camps resulting in the murder of more than half of all Hungarian Jews who, at the time of the German invasion, numbered 825,000, the largest remaining Jewish population in Europe and swollen by the numbers of Jewish refugees. By the end of the war, only 250,000 of them are estimated to have survived.

Eichmann's plan was to use 45 cattle cars per train, four trains a day, to deport 12,000 Jews from the countryside every day, starting in mid-May; this was to be followed by the deportation of Jews from Budapest from about 15th July. Between May and July 1944, all the people who had been declared to be Jewish because of religion or ancestry - over 434,000 Jews - were deported from the countryside on 147 trains, taken to Auschwitz and 80% of them gassed on arrival. This next photo shows Jews from Hungary arriving at Auschwitz.

https://en.wikipedia.org/wiki/File:Selection_on_the_ramp_at_Auschwitz-Birkenau,_1944_(Auschwitz_Album)_1b.jpg)
Selection on the ramp at Auschwitz, 1944

On 7th July, Horthy, the regent of Hungary, (following international pressure) ordered a halt to the deportations but by the time they had stopped three days later, nearly the entire community of Jews in the Hungarian countryside had gone. Laci's parents were among them. At the time of the German invasion in March 1944, Laci was stationed outside the provincial town of Diosgyor. After seeing the local Jewish population rounded up and deported, he wrote to his parents urging them to go to Budapest where he believed that it would be easier to hide or otherwise escape the roundup in a big city. But they did not take his advice. They were sent to Auschwitz and died there. His sister, Erzsike, was also sent to Auschwitz and survived by sewing military uniforms, but as the Russians advanced the Germans sent prisoners east to Germany. She was then sent to Belsen and died there of typhus on 17th March 1945. One of her friends survived and witnessed her death and was able to tell Laci what had happened to her.

Two ghettos were set up in Budapest and all Jews had to move into starred houses. There were frequent raids and mass executions but the Jews of Budapest escaped the systematic deportations which had by then been stopped. I've been to Budapest and seen the synagogue where many Jews lived and sought protection. It's a very small area and very moving.

Even after the end of the systematic deportations, the killing continued under the new puppet regime of Szalasi after Horthy was ousted in October 1944. In November 1944, the Germans rounded up 70,000 Jews in the brick yards in Budapest and forced them on a death march to Austria where they were then sent on to different extermination camps. Thousands were shot and thousands more died on the way. Between November 1944 and February 1945 the Arrow Cross militia men shot between ten and fifteen thousand Jews on the banks of the river Danube. Judy's cousin (one of the sons of her Uncle Izidor) took part in a courageous rescue operation when Jews were being taken to the Danube to be shot by uniformed Arrow Cross militia men. He and others like him dressed up in Arrow Cross uniforms and led at least some of the intended victims away from the scene, allowing them to escape. Judy didn't know what happened to her cousin afterwards, but Mary thinks they would probably have heard from him later, had he survived.

***

Judy was sent to Auschwitz and survived but all her family died. It's hard even now for me to believe that dear Judy had been through all of this. One morning the police came for them and ordered them to give up all their money, jewellery, pens, pencils and paper. Judy's group were marched to the railway station in a column five across, walking in the middle of the road, many of the locals looked on from the pavement and cheered. Mary says, *"Mami always felt very bitter about that"*. She went on to say that notwithstanding the generally good press the Hungarian government was given about their refusal to give up Jews until they were under direct occupation, *"my parents and all their friends have always insisted that the general public in Hungary was overwhelmingly anti-Semitic and endorsed everything which that was done against the Jews. For this reason they had very mixed feelings about the country of their birth and had little reluctance to leave when the opportunity arose"*.

At the station they boarded a train made up of cattle trucks. They travelled all night standing up because it was so crowded. Judy described how her father, who was diabetic, was dreadfully thirsty on the journey. They must have been among the last Jews sent to Auschwitz from Hungary. Judy told Mary that the journey took several days and that they arrived on 10th July 1944. It was on 7th July that under international pressure Horthy ordered the deportations to stop. Thousands were still sent on death marches to Austria but no longer to Auschwitz. On arrival "selections" were made and most were sent to their death in the gas chambers.

After six weeks in Auschwitz, Judy was transferred to Boizenburg near Hamburg where the SS had set up a satellite camp for women as part of the Neuengamme network of Nazi concentration camps. In all, 400 Jewish women from Hungary were transported from Auschwitz-Birkenau to Boizenburg. They had to work long shifts, day and night, for the company Thomsen & Co., producing and repairing parts for fighter planes and warships. Judy sometimes was so tired she fell asleep at the machinery which could have cut her arms off. She said that she kept herself going by thinking of her favourite classical music. They were on starvation rations but could smell the fried potatoes that were being cooked. She said that she was driven mad by the smell and swore that if she survived she would make sure to enjoy as many potato latkes as she could. As the war drew to a close they were force marched out by the camp staff (all of them female) while the bombing got worse.

In the meantime, Laci (known to Mary as Apu) was liberated from his forced labour camp earlier than Judy, on 20th December. Mary writes, *"Budapest was then still under German occupation, so he could not go straight home, but had to wait until the beginning of February. He had two stories to tell about the days just before liberation. One was a memory of waking up feeling lovely and warm one morning after sleeping in a school courtyard; the reason was a layer of thick snow which had fallen overnight and provided an extra layer on top of his blanket. The other story concerned one of his comrades who was a wealthy man and bribed the officers to let him sleep in a place where he thought he would be safe from the Allied bombing raids: despite this precaution this man was the only person in the camp to die in one of these raids".*

"Apu was also in touch with his Aunt Hermine in London, who told him she had heard about a Rona who had escaped to Switzerland, who could be his sister, Erzsike. Apu felt a little jealous about that possibility, he felt that his sister had managed things better than him, not for the first time. He found out later that Erzsike had in fact died in Belsen, just weeks before the war was over".

Now to Judy's liberation. The Boizenburg satellite camp was evacuated in April 1945 ahead of the advancing Allied troops. Mary has translated the handwritten journal which one of Judy's fellow prisoners kept of their journey home – over

1,100 kilometres from Boizenburg to Budapest. Days before the end of the war, the group of nine women (including Judy) were forced by their camp officers to march.

The journal begins on 28th April 1945, the night before the evacuation of the camp. Klara writes of the terrifying journey the small group made back to Budapest. They started under the orders of the German camp guards who disguised their camp uniforms and eventually threw all their weapons away. In the days that followed they were liberated by the US army but then had to be handed over to the Russians as it had been decided at Yalta that Hungary would fall under the Russian sphere of influence. The whole journey took weeks involving forced marches, rides on trucks, being crowded into train wagons, endless uncertainty, danger and the horror of destroyed towns and villages.

Mary writes, *"The tale told by the journal is appalling. More often than not, Mami and the others had to fend for themselves, fighting for food and shelter. They were forever waiting for the next transport to leave. Although so much of their time was spent waiting around they never dared to relax: they were constantly anxious a transport might leave without them. When they did manage to get on a transport, a truck or some wagons, it was usually overcrowded and very uncomfortable, nor did they have any real idea where they were in fact going. There were always rumours going round, followed by counter-rumours. No one ever knew anything for certain. At first the women kept their hopes up and maintained a positive attitude despite setbacks, but they were gradually reaching the end of their strength and their patience. Even the weather and the scenery they passed through seemed to reflect their mood. At first the diarist writes about lilacs blossoming and some beautiful sunny days, although she does talk about pouring rain and devastation as well. Later all we read about is cold, rain, ruins and filth everywhere and fellow passengers who are dirty, uncouth and selfish. All the women wanted was to get home in the hope of finding loved ones who had also survived, even Mami, who knew she was very unlikely to find any of her immediate family alive. On one occasion the diarist was told that her bad leg would have to be amputated unless she agreed to be hospitalised at once, but even this threat was not enough to detain her.*

It is amazing to me how the diarist found the energy to keep a journal in those circumstances. She records that they lost track of how many times they got on and off various trains. She did note down the names of many of the places they passed though many of them will have different names now and perhaps some are too small to appear on most maps. I have been able to find Stargard on the map, the place where the diarist says Mami and her friend Anci were squashed off a train by new people getting on. This incident is only mentioned briefly, so I presume they managed to get back on again. The diarist probably lost track of time too, because the only dated entry in the journal is the one right at the beginning, although she also mentions that when their train was passing through Tutz they learned that Germany had surrendered on 8 May. It certainly sounds as if the journey took several weeks".

In the end they arrived in Budapest on a train early in the morning. The diary describes them seeing the zoo, a railway bridge, and the Nyugati Palyaudvar railway station. Mary writes, "The final words of the journal are 'Ila val hazaerkeztunk', Ila and I have arrived home. I find these words deeply moving, no matter how many times I read them. I try to imagine how Mami must have felt at that moment". Mary also says, "There is a photo of Mami taken in June 1945, which I think she needed for an identity card, that shows something of her physical and emotional state at this time". All her Hungarian family had died in the camps except one cousin, and two uncles and an aunt who had gone to America.

I've always believed that there was something fairytale-like about Judy having been restored to her young man, Laci. And, of course, it was extraordinary but when we went to the Jewish museum in Llubjana I learned to think of it differently. In the museum there was a video of an old man talking about his family. When he was a small boy his nanny had saved his life. One night, the Gestapo came and took his parents away but as they struggled his nanny swept him up from his bed and climbed out onto the roof with him and got to some neighbours over the rooftops. She hid him for the rest of the war. After the war he went to school and he was the only Jewish boy there, all the rest were gone. One day when he was 11, his nanny told him that she'd received a letter to say that his mother had survived the camps and was coming home. They were due to meet in the park. As this now old man described the meeting, he cried and could hardly speak. He saw across the park a hunched old woman who was very thin and didn't look as he remembered her at all. She hugged him tight but he felt that he didn't know her. On watching this old man in tears, I had to go and sit outside the museum and I sobbed. I realised only then as I listened to him talking just how very difficult the reunion between Laci and Judy must have been with so much terrible experience behind them and so much loss. None of us can really understand what others have been through. I thought I'd understood but I hadn't at all. I look at the family tree and realise that on that side of the family at least, there is no extended family living a life I just don't know about. They were all slaughtered. Judy and her friend got "home" but there was no family home or members left.

On reading Mary's notes, I find that the reunion of Laci and Judy was in fact even more extraordinary. Laci and Judy were very keen on each other before the war but his family didn't approve because her family, the Fernbachs, had lost all their money in the Great Crash and were considered to be too poor.

Mary writes, *"My mother was 7 years younger than my Dad. Before the war her family lived in Kispest, a suburb of Budapest. Her family came from Kolomyya, now in Ukraine. She worked at the same textile factory as my Dad and they also mixed in the same circles socially. They dated quite seriously in the early 40s but my Dad called it off mainly because his family was against it- my mother came from a poorer background and they thought he would be taking on responsibility for supporting her whole family financially. This was a very hard time economically"*.

So Laci and Judy separated and during the war Judy married another man, Dr Arato, with the same first name (Laszlo or Laci) as our Laci. They had only been married a few months when they were deported to Auschwitz together with their families. After a few weeks they were both sent to separate camps. Judy survived but her family and her husband did not. When she finally made it back to Budapest she and the first Laci got together again and they married in 1946. So their reunion must have been even more extraordinary and poignant than I'd even imagined.

Mary writes, *"One day Mami saw Apu in the street. Her heart beat faster, but she didn't go up to him or talk to him. Apu had a half share in a property in Kispest he had bought with Imre and when he went to look at the house he also called on the Zadors to see what fate had befallen them. (I have already mentioned that the Zadors were friends of Apu's family too.) Apu had already ascertained that in Rakosszentmihaly only a handful of Jews were left of a community of several hundreds. The Zadors were pleased to see him and said he should go and see Mami, who was working in her shop. He told me more than once the words he spoke to Mami on this occasion: 'Most mar sohase engedjuk el egymas kezet.' 'From now on we're never going to let go of each other's hand.'"*.

It will have been a quiet, and very small, wedding with both sorely feeling the loss of so many of their families and, as with my grandparents' wedding, there were no photographs. Mary writes, *"The marriage took place at a Budapest registry office on 25 May 1946, with Apu's uncle Imre and Mami's brother-in-law Jancsi Halasz as witnesses. There are no wedding photos: it must have been a quiet affair and they must have both felt the absence of their closest family"*. Laci told Mary, *"that day was the happiest day of his life"*.

The Ronas in Budapest post war and escape across the border in 1956

Laci and Judy made a decent life in spite of the poverty and hardship after the war. They lived in Budapest and had two children, Maria (Mary), born in 1947, and Gabor (Raymond), born in 1953.

Laci and Judy had originally planned to leave Hungary shortly after the war and had submitted applications to emigrate to Israel but Judy was reluctant to go with a new baby and since Laci was doing well in business they decided to stay. But events overtook them. Laci had joined the communist party but was expelled as a bourgeois entrepreneur. It was hard to find work and pay was poor so he was running out of savings. Mary recalls Laci saying that he never had money to buy more than three days' food. Life became increasingly dangerous and they started the safety measure of family and friends ringing the doorbell twice so as to avoid panic as a ring on the doorbell in the night (as happened once and terrified the family but turned out to be a friend) usually meant being sent to Siberia. Mary explains that they kept this custom going right up until Laci's death in 2000. In fact, I realise that when I went to visit Laci not that long before his death, I was unaware of this custom and will have blithely rung the doorbell.

After the end of the Second World War, Hungary had been put under the Soviet sphere of influence and the regime was Stalinist. The Hungarian Revolution (also known as the Hungarian Uprising) started in October 1956 with protests objecting to Russian Stalinist geopolitical domination of Hungary. Soon, there was fighting across the country.

Then on 4th November 1956, events forced the situation when Russian tanks rolled in to crush the revolution, resulting in the death of 2,500 Hungarians, the imprisonment of 22,000 people, and huge numbers of refugees escaping the country. I remember when we visited Budapest in 1986, the buildings were still significantly damaged by bullet holes.

My father had by then been working in Germany as a foreign correspondent for two years. I have a letter he wrote to his mother about the events. He'd met the wife of a *Sunday Times* journalist based in Budapest. She talked to him about being part of a group hiding in the British Embassy for several days. He writes of his sense of horror at the Russians mowing down Hungarians in the street not all that far from where he was living.

The Ronas must have been terrified. Within weeks they walked out over the border holding the hands of their two children, aged nine and three, and carrying a suitcase. They were among the 200,000 people (20,000 of them Jews) who fled the country.

Mary has written a very powerful piece about their escape. This is the story of so many refugees, people all over the world and huge numbers of them today. Again, I am including that verbatim account in the Appendices and it makes very powerful reading. As I read it I keep thinking that all of this was happening only months after I was born in Germany where my father was working as a foreign correspondent covering the news for the *Daily Telegraph*.

Laci and Judy had mixed feelings. Whilst they were sympathetic with the aims of the communists (who had also suppressed antisemitism), times were hard (Laci was a businessman but private enterprise was forbidden so his monthly salary was barely enough to buy food) and it was plain that antisemitism was still very present. Since they had no family left after the Holocaust there were no compelling family reasons to stay. They received a telegram from my grandmother in Brentwood who was concerned about their safety and invited them to come and stay. They'd also had a letter inviting them to stay from the youngest of the Reichenfeld seven, Laci's sister, Hermine, who had long since settled in London like her brother, Miksa. There were also relatives in America. Laci had briefly been a member of the communist party so he might well not have been welcome in America. They decided to get to England.

The Rona family in 1956: Laci, Judy, Mary and Gabriel taken for their immigration papers to England

They finally left on 15th December leaving behind their home and everything they knew taking what they could carry. Mary was nine and Raymond was only three. They had to borrow money to pay for a guide to help take them across the border. Mary recalls

Judy teaching them how to make the sign of the cross and her feeling very anxious about being Jewish. They took the train to Gyor where they met their guide. It's strange to think that Gyor is where all the Reichenfeld family had settled two centuries before and where, after the war, there were none left.

They caught another train but had to switch from passenger carriages to goods trucks, which was, as Mary points out, *"for Mami certainly not a new experience"*. Chilling. And there was a terrifying moment when Judy and Raymond got off the train too soon and nearly got left behind.

They left in the morning but it was dark when they completed the train element of the journey. From there they had to walk for hours and then catch a boat which had been sabotaged by the Russians to cross the big lake which separates Hungary and Austria. This is the terrifying experience of refugees both then and today. Mary writes:

"By the time we got off the train at Hegyko, darkness had fallen. From here we had to go on foot to the shore of Lake Ferto (known as the Neusiedlersee on the Austrian side) where two boats were waiting to take us across the lake to the other side of the border. (NB The border with Austria goes down the middle of the lake.) Apu was carrying Raymond as well as luggage: it was all getting too heavy for him and he ended up ditching one of the cases he had been carrying. I wonder if anyone found it and made good use of whatever we had in it. Mami, for her part, twisted her ankle and had to lean on me for the rest of the trek. When we finally reached the boats, we found the Russians had shot holes into them, so that people had to take turns to bail out the water coming in through them. Another problem was that when we had got into the boats it was found that there were too many people in the boat our family had chosen to get into. The guides said two people would have to get out and move to the other boat. No one would budge, everyone was in family groups. Apu broke the stalemate by agreeing to get into the other boat with me. I think I went to sleep on

Apu's arm. There was a thick mist and it took us six hours to find what we hoped was the right spot on the Austrian side. A bonfire was lit and eventually we were spotted and taken to a refugee camp near Eisenstadt. Almost immediately I started being sick and was taken to a hospital in the town. There was no physical cause for my sickness, it was more due to my emotional state after our adventures. It was while I was being sick that I tasted my first banana – tropical fruit that would have had to be imported had not been available in Hungary. I could not keep the banana down and have never been able to eat bananas since. In the hospital I received a package that had been prepared by the WVS: it contained a handkerchief, a ball-point pen and a pad of paper among other things. I also got a pair of booties from somewhere – I think the shoes I had been wearing had been done in on our long walk to the boats. I was at an impressionable age and have always remembered this rather low point in our lives, when we were dependent on others for the basics of existence, with hardly anything we could call our own. You can have a secure existence one minute and the next find yourself a refugee in need of food and shelter – it isn't something that only happens to other people and refugees are not a strange alien species".

When they got to Vienna where they had to apply for admission to the UK, Laci's old boss offered him a job in Austria but that was far too near to Hungary for him. He was determined to get to London. They did get there and moved in with Hermine. Mary recalls her being very critical of Judy's neat appearance saying that no one went to the hairdresser in England in those days and everyone had to work. There seems to be something very telling about this. If you're a refugee, you're likely to take some of your best clothes and it's important to maintain your dignity and try to create a good impression to show that you're a person with a life. So to be criticised for trying to look smart reveals how little those of us who have not had to live through this can really understand.

Mary writes, *"Aunt Hermine was then 77, lonely, and no doubt embittered by much that had happened to her. It was unfortunate that her first impression of Mami was so mistaken. Mami worked just as hard at everything else as she did on her appearance. She looked like a film star and she always aimed for perfection in everything she did"*.

Mary describes remembering buying their first English clothes at Marks and Spencer in Kilburn but also explains that her parents continued to wear the clothes they'd managed to bring from Hungary. They'd carefully selected their best quality clothes and *"on the occasion of our son David's bar mitzvah Apu looked very smart in the suit he had worn when we escaped from Hungary nearly forty years earlier"*.

I remember Judy as a very neat person. Mary remembers that the taps were always gleaming and the parquet floor freshly polished. She recalls a friend in Budapest saying that if a fly ventured into their flat it would "slip on the parquet". They established a new life but it was hard. It was, for instance, difficult to find work when neither of Laci or Judy spoke English. He worked for various companies starting work as a packer, then as a warehouse assistant and was eventually promoted to production manager and buyer at Lana Knit. In time, Judy became a homebased saleswoman for their clothes too. After some years they moved to the house I remember visiting: 46 St George's Road in Golders Green.

One of the things the family had to get used to was overcoming the fear of persecution for being Jewish. Understandably Mary writes about this a good deal given what her parents had been through and their anxiety not to reveal their backgrounds. She describes one of Laci's cousins, Harry, who also moved to London but who they could have no contact with as he never revealed to his own children that he was Jewish. He didn't even want them to know that he was Hungarian and it was only after his death in 1981 that they discovered the truth.

Mary also explains that Laci was baptised when he was in the forced labour camp because the Swiss offered a degree of protection to the detainees but only if they converted. Of course, this was not a new phenomenon at all and for many hundreds of years Jews have either been forced to convert or chosen to do it to protect themselves. Laci was apparently anxious that Judy should also be baptised, which she did, but she refused to attend the classes. They christened Mary but never made any pretence of being Christian and Mary explains that, unlike many others, she always knew that she was Jewish but for years at school she and her parents were anxious to keep this secret. Mary told me that it's thanks to my grandparents that she went to Henrietta Barnett School in Hampstead Garden Suburb as this is where my grandparents lived and was the school that both my mother and Aunty Janet had been to. Even there the fact that she was Jewish was something she kept secret for a long time even after it became apparent that half the girls were also Jewish. It was through friends there that Mary did become religious and explained her background. Mary became orthodox Jewish and married the son of a rabbi while her brother became an evangelical Christian. She explains the complexity of faith and fear of persecution well.

I think now is a good moment to reflect on so many members of the family who rejected Judaism and why. My grandparents became atheists, my mother never admitted to her close friend that she was Jewish, Granny didn't know that she was Jewish until she was an adult and apart from telling me that, she never talked about any of this either. I inherited money from the widow of one of my Russian grandfather's nephews who had refused her husband any contact with his family but seems to have regretted it and left money to the survivors of his long lost cousins. Laci was baptised. Mary writes that her parents had strong but ambivalent feelings about being Jewish, and that *"it would not take much genius to see how suffering extreme persecution might make you feel negative about the aspect of yourself you were being persecuted for and yet at one and the same time give you a close bond with those who have shared your fate"*.

The history of my family did not involve the same suffering but there was secrecy there too. My grandparents rejected Judaism and became atheists but I suspect that was because of family rejection (and that Granny had never been brought up Jewish) rather than out of fear. The death of Marguerite before the planned double wedding may also have shaken their belief. I don't know because it was not talked about. I started writing this family history believing that my grandfather had also had the experience of escaping persecution as a small child and although I've now discovered that this is not true, his father did leave Russia along with many others. They will have been well aware of the waves of pogroms which resulted in the growing community of Jews in Middlesbrough and throughout the UK.

My grandparents allowed their two daughters to adopt whatever religion they chose and they both became Christian. Janet became a lay preacher but my mother never really believed in religion and didn't like attending church. My father always said that he was really pleased to have the Jewish connection and I recall Mummy saying how much she'd enjoyed going to Mary's children's weddings in Manchester where the women danced on one side of a partition and the men on the other. She found it joyous and very liberating. So it's interesting that my mother had a nose job done possibly because of anti-Semitic tropes about the appearance of Jews. Also, only recently and well after my mother's death, I learned from her great friend, Jane Asser (who she went to university with, and they shared both a flat and their joint 21st birthday party), that she had had no idea that Mummy came from a Jewish family.

A history of fear and sadness will probably have played a good part in that silence. My grandmother always said that she didn't believe in thinking about the past or keeping anything old. Always onwards, only the present and the future. I can remember Mummy saying that she always felt how incredibly lucky her family had been to be living in England during the war and how very close they had been to being caught up in the Holocaust. And when I think about it she may well have known far more about her family than she was ever willing to tell me. Certainly we as a family never discussed any of this even though we did discuss religion (she became Christian but she always made it clear that she didn't believe in the central tenets and only came to church at Christmas). I can also see from my father's letters to my mother in 1955, while they were engaged when he was based in Bonn in Germany as a foreign correspondent and she was working in London, that he wrote a good deal about the aftermath of the war and how much both the Germans and the English knew about the Holocaust but failed to act. As historians, as a journalist and as a young couple who started their married lives in Germany, they are bound to have thought about it all but the silences were still there when it came to something so close to the family.

I feel very proud to be related to the Rona family and to have the chance to tell their story here. I feel very lucky that it was not the story of my own family.

Laci and Judy were at our wedding in 1981. Laci had yet more sadness after this. Judy suffered from depression and died of cancer in 1992 after 46 years of married life together and their son, Raymond, also died young of cancer, leaving three young children. I often wondered how Laci managed to be so resilient and cheerful after all of this. He told me that the best thing was to go for a walk every day and to enjoy tea and cake.

Laci was 89 when he died in May 2000. I went to see him not that long before and we had tea at his house on St George's Road. I'd never talked to him before about the past but I decided to ask him what he believed in at this stage in his long life. He told me that he could not believe in religion at all. He told me that, although he had Judy, they'd both lost sisters, brothers, parents, aunts, uncles, cousins, everyone they loved, in the camps. He believed in "now", not the past or the promises of religion. He held my hand tight, looked at me hard and smiled, saying, 'What I believe in is the present. I believe in now, that you are here having tea with me and holding my hand and that is wonderful.'

These are some of the silences, the gaps and the overlaps in my family history. They play an important part of who I feel I am. They always have. The story of escape from persecution and the sense that England used to be a safe haven for refugees (and is no longer) is very important to my identity and what I care about.

I can understand why these silences were kept, the sense of "don't look back, live now". And I feel the importance of holding hands across these silences. I recall Laci holding my hand at our wedding and again holding it tight when I met him not very long before he died. As Laci said when he and Judy were reunited after the war, 'Most mar sohase engedjuk el egymas kezet' – 'From now on we're never going to let go of each other's hand.'

I've already arrived in this history thanks to the photo of me in Brentwood with the Rona children recently arrived – in my case from Germany and in theirs from Hungary. So now is the right moment to bring in my parents. It is through them that hands were joined between Lancashire, Russia, and Hungary (or rather London, where my maternal grandparents were then living). But before I do that I want to write a piece about my mother's cousin (the only one she ever knew and the one I met). Dennis Bloodworth with his Hungarian Jewish background moved to Singapore, was married to Chinese Ching Ping who had escaped communist China with nothing and who together went on to adopt her orphaned nephews who I also knew as a child. The chronology is striking. In 1956: the Ronas escaped Hungary, I was born, and Dennis moved to Singapore with Ching Ping.

This next section will complete the diaspora and the geographical and cultural spread of my family before I go back to my parents.

5. Singapore and Dennis Bloodworth and Liang Ching Ping

I remember Dennis very well. He was my mother's favourite cousin. Although he lived in Singapore for nearly 50 years, they were close and wrote and visited often. He was a tall man with a big head, kind eyes and a very gentle manner, nice to one and all and always with a very good sense of humour. Everyone in the family was very fond of him and indeed there was a certain rivalry as to who had heard from him most recently or who had been to visit him in Singapore.

Dennis was my grandmother's nephew, the son of her eldest sister, Rosalie, by her first marriage. She was the most Hungarian of the family who lived, when I knew her, in St John's Wood in a flat with her Chihuahua. I can see Dennis in her flat – rather too large for the setting and making everyone smile as he told a funny story. He was not only very nice but also the most exotic of the family because he lived in Singapore with his Chinese wife, Liang Ching Ping, and their three Chinese children, her orphaned nephews who they'd adopted. He was also the member of my mother's family who my parents liked best. As a boy, he'd spent a lot of time with the Bentleys and was treated as a brother. When Mummy worked as an au pair in Paris she was befriended by Dennis and his first wife. And as a fellow journalist, Daddy admired him and loved talking to him. We had his books on our shelves, they went to stay with him in Singapore, and we used to have his sons, Bosco and John, to lunch at our house in Kenley. When Dennis was mentioned, a letter arrived or a visit was planned, there was always a sense of anticipation and a smile on the face. So, although he lived such a long way away, Dennis was always a close and much loved part of the family.

Born in 1919, Dennis was only seven when his father divorced his mother (he explains that his mother said that he had died but as

Dennis says, kids know better). Dennis had to leave school early in 1936 when he was 17 when his mother divorced her second husband and they were left penniless. He did all kinds of jobs including working as a pig food analyst and as a cub reporter writing obituaries but when he was 20, World War Two broke out and he spent the next seven years in the army tramping through North Africa, Sicily, Italy and Hungary under the Russians. In 1946, he married a Hungarian girl in Budapest (where his mother, Rosalie, had been born) and was promptly demobbed for fraternising with the enemy. Back in London he became the office manager of a sheet metal plant in Peckham that went bust under his management in 1949.

After this he managed to get a job for the *Observer* newspaper through an introduction to the editor, David Astor, who read a test piece Dennis had written. 'Astor shook his head sadly and said that unfortunately he could not possibly offer him a job. My heart sank like a pebble. Unless, of course, I was prepared to go to Paris.' Dennis worked there for five and a half years during which time his wife left him. After his first marriage broke up he was sent to Saigon to cover the end of the first Indochina war after the French were defeated in 1954.

He arrived in Saigon in early 1955 when the war in Indochina was about to enter its next phase, the Vietnam War. In April that year, the Vietnamese National Army launched an attack on Saigon which lasted until May, leaving 500 people dead and 20,000 homeless. It was also in 1955 that the USA first got involved in Vietnam by supporting the South Vietnamese against North Vietnam which was, in turn, supported by Mao Zedong and Stalin.

Saigon was Vietnam's second largest city and had been the capital of French Indochina from 1887 to 1902 and then again from 1945 until the French withdrew their military and evacuated in 1954. It is known for its well-preserved French colonial architecture and even now in the street markets there are elements of French cuisine. I assume it made sense for Dennis to go there given that he spoke good French after living in Paris. He arrived at an extraordinary time, interviewing all manner of people including a Trotskyite turned Buddhist sage and paint salesman and royal courtiers and princelings, many of whom appear in his books.

But it was in July 1955 that his life changed when he managed to get a visa to visit China, the first journalist to be allowed into Mao Zedong's communist China. He was told the visa would only be valid if he entered China at Shenzen on the border with Hong Kong on 16th July (the day I was born just one year later). So he flew to Hong Kong on 7 July 1955 and it was quite by chance that he there met his future wife, Liang Ching Ping. A contact suggested they go out in a foursome and Dennis, who had only just arrived after flying overnight and had a great deal to do, nearly couldn't be bothered but for some reason he did decide to go.

Ping and Dennis fell for each other immediately. He was a six-foot tall Anglo Hungarian who'd lived in London and Paris. She was a five-foot-four Confucian living then hand to mouth, bringing up her three orphaned nephews by selling pigeons and working illegally as an unregistered schoolteacher. They only had nine days together before he had to go to China, where he spent the next six weeks, but before he left he proposed to her. They went dancing and she writes in the book they wrote 42 years later, "Dennis asked me if I was happy. I said I thought I could fly. So fly now, he cried, and suddenly held me up high, floating in the air, flying gently to the clouds, heaven and earth spinning round and round". I love the image of tall Dennis whirling petite Ping high in the air.

There were immediately family objections on both sides. He wrote, "Her family were horrified at the very idea of her wedding a pink and white 'red-haired barbarian' and promptly ostracized her for five years. On my side, my mother was furious, and even a favourite aunt wrote to me saying simply, 'Don't, Dennis, don't do it!'" But they were a strong couple and they went ahead anyhow. Dennis wrote, "At precisely 2pm on 12 March 1957 at the Supreme Court Registry Office in Singapore we both married barbarians". (The favourite aunt must have been my grandmother who also, of course, had objected to my father. This may also have been something which brought my parents and Dennis together).

Why did we in England call her Judy when Dennis always called her by her real name, Ping? She actually never took an English name but at the age of five she was nicknamed "Zhu-Di" by her mother when she'd been particularly naughty. It means "tomboy of the Pearl River" and this resulted in her Anglicised name Judy. Whereas I only ever knew her as Judy, I will call her Ping as it's clear that this was her name to all of her own family.

Dennis and Ping came from such incredibly different backgrounds and cultures but found a harmonious way of life together in their lovely bungalow in Singapore. He had to spend many years travelling and working across Asia and loved it, always going over everything with Ping to make sure he had properly reflected the Chinese approach and had understood the highly complex intricacies of Chinese politics.

He was a distinguished and respected journalist. He was the highly regarded Far East correspondent for the *Observer* newspaper from 1956 to 1981. He published what was the first major work on China, *The Chinese Looking Glass*, which became a best-seller and it is said that when Richard Nixon went to China in 1972 he took the book with him and "changed the balance of world power" according to the *Independent* newspaper's obituary. He was given an OBE in 1989. The British government suggested appointing him as high commissioner to Britain but neither he nor Ping wanted the job. They wanted a quieter more peaceful life together. Both of them loved writing.

He wrote a lot of books, many of them bestsellers. He believed that books should not be dry and academic but "fit for human consumption". He wrote 18 books altogether, most were political, some funny, some thrillers, most are dedicated to his wife, Liang Ching Ping, to whom he said he felt "an unrepayable debt". One of these dedications is the Lao proverb, "When you have heard you must listen, when you have seen you must judge in your heart".

He died in Singapore in 2005 when he was 86. The funeral and wake were attended by Singapore dignitaries and no doubt many journalists as well. Among the political attendees (so the *Independent* reported in his obituary) was Lee Kuan Yew who had been Singapore's first prime minister and served between 1959 and 1990, known as the "founding genius" of what became the gleaming but authoritarian island state of Singapore today.

I always knew Dennis was a successful journalist but now that I've done my research I see that he wore his fame lightly. We, the family, saw a different man to the one who was close to so much international and geopolitical complexity. The man we knew was funny and affectionate and this is the man who emerges in the book he and his wife, Liang Ching Ping, wrote together called *I Married a Barbarian*. They had already co-written two books about China but this one was about their lives together. It was published in 2001 when he was 82 and she was in her late 70s. I have to say that I've only just read it and I greatly enjoyed it. It's a lovely book exploring the two immensely different cultures they came from and they talk with such love and affection and humour about one another and their "barbarian" ways. They each write their perspective on their lives, food, culture, democracy, Confucian and Taoist ideals, geopolitics – each using humour and affection. (Even this book has a review on the back page by the president of Singapore between 1985 and 1993, Wee Kim Wee, who had known them for 40 years when the book was published and clearly liked both them and the book very much).

I only met Judy once when she visited England in 1965 when I was nine. I remember her being very lovely-looking, rather fierce and very independently-minded. Reading the book I think I would have liked her a lot had I known her as an adult.

Her life went through many remarkably different phases. First the wealthy ancestral home, then the years of revolution and war, then exile and poverty in Hong Kong, finally meeting Dennis and settling with him in Singapore.

She was born Ching Ping in Beijing into the proud Liang family, wealthy landowning and strictly Confucian. She described her ancestral home in South Guangdong province as "a walled maze of courtyards and moongates and pavilions where four generations of the Liang family with their wives, concubines and children, a hierarchy of 500 souls in all (I was Seventeenth Son's Eighth Daughter) were waited on hand and foot every step of the day by almost as many servants. At the entrance were great double doors, and inside, the Ancestral Hall with incense bearing altar and ranks of red and gold tablets commemorating distinguished dead of the family". Her grandmother had bound feet and never left the walls of the ancestral home.

A FAMILY TREE

Her father was a civil servant and became Sun Yat-sen's confidential secretary in 1917, later running several prefectures under his leadership. Sun Yat-sen was the leader of the revolution which overthrew the Quing dynasty. He became the first president of the Republic of China and the first leader of the Kuomintang (the Nationalist Party of China). Ping's father worked hard and died in office at the age of 53. He wanted his daughters to become professionals. One became a doctor and Ping became a teacher having studied at Zhong Shan University.

Two of her brothers became Kuomintang generals in the army of Sun Yat-Sen's successor, Chiang Kai-shek. They fought for many years first in the long war following Japan's invasion and then in the fight against the communists. The Kuomintang governed most of China until it was defeated in the civil war by Mao Zedong's communists in 1949. When the Kuomintang lost, the brothers and their family were disgraced and lost everything. The leadership (including Chiang Kai-Shek), the remaining army and their supporters, two million in all, fled to Taiwan but the brothers stayed behind. The eldest was publicly tried and killed, the two sisters were publicly persecuted and both ended up committing suicide.

Ping's mother had already left for Hong Kong, taking her sister's three boys to safety where Ping soon went to join them. "My life was full of utter helplessness and contradiction, the future grim. But my mother said, 'Poverty is not guilt, so not a thing to be afraid of.' And I clung to that". As Dennis wrote, "When Seventeenth Son's Eighth Daughter, born with a jade spoon in her mouth, arrived in Kowloon, Hong Kong in 1949, it was like the end of the known world".

Her mother was from a poor family and knew how to manage so she made ends meet by breeding pigeons for sale and Ping got some work as a tutor. But in 1952 her mother went to join the rest of the family in Taiwan where there were seven other grandchildren. Somehow Ping had to feed and raise her three orphaned nephews. The Catholic Church agreed to take the boys on as boarders in Macau and she carried on working as a teacher. Dennis and Ping always treated the boys as their family and in 1968 Dennis and Ping were allowed to adopt Dominic, Bosco and John when they were 14, 12 and 9.

I never met the eldest, Dominic, but I knew both Bosco and his wife, Alice, and John and his wife, Ivy. They all went to English universities and all lived in Europe for about ten years before they each decided to move back to Singapore. Bosco was a laboratory chemist and John was an accountant. All three brothers and their wives moved back to Singapore in due course.

I love the idea of their Singapore lives. I wish I'd been to visit. I know that my parents very much liked their bungalow and gardens which were laid out over three levels. Dennis describes the "Chinese Tower of Babel" he lived in with each of their sons marrying a Chinese girl from three different countries, each speaking different dialects: Dominic's wife, a Hokkien from Taiwan, Bosco's, a Chaozhou from Hong Kong, and John's, a Hakka from Singapore. He writes that Ping always used to say that she and Dennis both spoke each other's language so badly that they couldn't quarrel.

Ping came to England twice only. I remember the first time in 1965. The second time was in 1998 when they celebrated their wedding anniversary by getting remarried in St Paul's Cathedral in the OBE chapel.

She writes about the English appreciation of sunshine. "When no actual rain, it is 'good weather', and if they see the sun they are delighted and shout 'lovely day' to everyone". She writes very poetically about their trip to Oxford in 1998 with my parents. Daddy took them to visit his old college, New College, where she said she felt at home. Over the stone doorway was the inscription of the founder, William of Wykeham, "Manners Maketh Man". "'Cannot be more Confucian,' I cried and insisted to take a photo there with both of us". And when it came to punting, she wrote of my mother, "When Valerie took over the long pole and brought the boat forward, gliding smoothly on the surface in the more open water, she stood very straight in the stern, looking exactly like a statue made of bronze, everything still, only a pair of hanging earrings in the breeze beside her face". Mummy loved her long earrings.

Their book is full of so much wisdom and interest but what I love best is the sense of two people who learned to get the best out of life together, who loved each other, made each other laugh and who grew old gracefully. Ping writes, "Now the mood like rosy clouds in evening sky. We have come out of intense emotion of past to go into the quieter life, live in peace with each other, walking slowly hand in hand in silence after supper to enjoy the breeze and admire the night, I feel I drank glass wine and forget my small feet altogether."

At the end of their book, Dennis wrote how they held hands tightly during their remarriage vows. "We knew the secret of a long marriage. It was an open mind, a shedding of all preconceived ideas, a refusal to listen to what others said, a rejection of all the misinformed dogma propagated by the pundits about each other's people. And we held the proof." And Ping wrote, "Since more than 40 years passed, we still have a marriage based on nine days acquaintance. Even 40 years on I feel like bride, my heart beating fast."

Here is the front cover of their book, *I Married a Barbarian*. I knew Dennis without a mustache but even with it they both look like film stars. The back page includes quotes from the former president of Singapore and the *South China Morning Post* both praising it.

Dennis Bloodworth and Liang Ching Ping on the front cover of their book, "I married a barbarian"

6. My parents: Lancashire, London and Germany

And so we come to my parents and the joining of these two very different families, the Hopes and the Bentleys. John Michael Hope married Valerie Frances Bentley on 10th September 1955.

When I think of my parents I think of us on holiday driving long distances, putting up the tent (often in the rain), Daddy making Mummy laugh, and the two of them playing *Scrabble* at night by the Campingaz lamp, with Mark and me tucked up in our sleeping bags.

My parents on their wedding day 12th September 1955

My father, Michael Hope, has already made his appearance, born on 21st January 1928. Since his birth certificate states that he was born in Woodplumpton, he must have been born at home as it's only a small village – certainly with no hospital. After the terrible loss of the last baby, this will have been a joyous birth. My grandmother was evidently in a bit of a daze as he was meant to be named Michael Joseph, the second name being his father's, but when she filled in the form she wrote John Michael Hope instead. And so he became J.M. Hope of the many practised signatures in which the J, the M, and the H all became part of one illegible but highly recognisable scrawl. And although he was always meant to be called Michael (and was indeed called Michael by everyone except for some of his school friends who named him Bob after the famous film actor, Bob Hope) the name John caused all kinds of official difficulties. For instance, in the NHS, he was always known as John Hope which I only discovered when trying to track him down once in hospital after some emergency in his old age, only to be told repeatedly, to my dismay, that there was no Michael Hope in the hospital.

My grandparents were clearly so overjoyed at the birth of a healthy baby that they went straight on to give my father a sister, Mary, in February 1930. This family photo must have been taken

My grandparents S.E. and Joseph Hope with my father, Michael, and my aunt Mary not long before Joseph died of appendicitis

only a few months before their father, Joseph, died. After this, no more photos were taken until the children were much older. The next to appear are these studio photographs taken when they were six and four, I should guess. What a lot of years of trauma and sadness.

A studio portrait of Mary and Michael Hope

Here is the house he grew up in, Broomfield in Leigh.

Broomfield, St Helen's Road, Leigh, Lancashire, where my father grew up

Meanwhile only a few months later, down in London, my mother, Valerie Frances Bentley, was born on 18th May 1930. This photo shows my grandmother, Jo Bentley, with baby Valerie. I like the second one of my mother as a small girl on the beach. She was always happy near water.

My mother, Valerie, with her mother, Jo, and on the beach

I don't know why the names Valerie and Michael were chosen but the names Frances and Joseph were important family names on both sides although, of course, the two young families in Lancashire and London then had no idea that they would become further entwined when my parents married. Joseph is the name shared by my maternal great-great-grandparents Jozsef and Jozsefa, my maternal grandfather, Frank Joseph Bentley, my maternal grandmother, Josephine Bentley, and my paternal grandfather, Joseph Hope, with the odd twist that my father was mistakenly named John instead of Joseph. The name Frances shared by my maternal grandfather (Francis always known as Frank), my mother (her second name), my paternal grandmother (Frances

Prescott), my great aunt (also Frances Prescott), and my father's sister, Mary (her second name). And the names have been continued. Frances is my second name and the family tradition was passed on to our daughter, Frances. My brother Mark's second name is Joseph and my cousin is called Jo.

I like to think of my parents growing up in very different places, neither having any idea about the other, and yet inexorably moving towards one another. I encouraged my father to write about his childhood growing up in mining Lancashire in the 1930s and although he didn't get very far I'm lucky to be able to use his notes to fill out what I knew about those years. Also, Granny never moved again so I knew the house he grew up in whereas the Bentleys moved quite a lot. I have rather less to go on with my mother. She died on her 73rd birthday before I got into family history and hadn't asked all the questions I now wish I had.

Daddy grew up in Leigh after the family moved there from Woodplumpton. He describes how regular life was with meals at the same time every day. They always had the full breakfast with porridge. They called lunch "dinner" as it was the main meal of the day and had meat and two or three veg and then pudding. Tea was at four o'clock when they had sandwiches and cake. Supper was at 6:30pm when they had sardines or beans on toast, Welsh rarebit (melted cheese on toast) or something more Lancashire traditional such as pigs' trotters as Granny didn't like brains or tripe. Some food was delivered. For instance, the milk which was brought in a horse-drawn float and served out of a large churn by the local farmer's wife. And my father describes bread being delivered in an ancient motor van "just like the one in *Dad's Army*".

In his memoire, my father wrote about his Uncle Rupert who owned a large car and used to take them for a ride in the summer to the sands near Southport where cars were allowed on the beach. For Christmas they went to Uncle Rupert and Aunt Maud's for a huge turkey and all the trimmings and on New Year's Day they had Uncle Harold and Aunt Ada to tea. He wrote that there were lots of parties at Christmastime including fancy dress parties such as the occasion when Granny rented a room at the Rope and Anchor

Hotel and dressed my father as a Dutchman with wooden clogs, which he said he hated because he wanted to go as an admiral.

Children also spent a lot of time being ill with what Daddy calmly describes as the "usual childish ailments – chickenpox, mumps, measles, whooping cough and scarlet fever". He said he quite enjoyed being tucked up ill in bed as nice Dr Tickle, who only lived three doors away, would come by and Aunt Frances who read to him. He particularly remembers being read *Wind in the Willows*. And when I was a child and also ill in bed for quite a long time, I remember Daddy reading it to me too.

When he was five he started school at Miss Bowker's where he sat in a large class where they all sat on long benches. What he remembered best was finding a German stamp in the gutter on his walk to school. He says it was "overprinted 150 million marks". His mother said it was worth nothing which was true because it was from the period of Germany's hyper-inflation between the wars but my father insisted on keeping it and it became the first in his lifelong collection of stamps from all over the world and with a particular line in German stamps (I still have a huge number of his albums and will one day get them valued).

After that he went to Leigh Church of England junior school where they played marbles and conkers – one child with a conker threaded on a string tries to break the other child's chestnut by swinging it viciously. He described being badly bullied. He wrote, "I remember being wrestled to the ground and pummelled by two boys, Eddie Foulkes and John Dickinson, at the instigation of two girls who watched with glee from a window at the treatment I received". Luckily, he had a cousin at the school who was tougher and bigger and he made sure this didn't happen again.

He recalls two great trips. One to see the Queen Mary transatlantic liner in Southampton from a holiday in Bournemouth when a friend lent them her flat. And an exciting trip to Blackpool when they took a flight from the airfield around Blackpool Tower at the same time as Amy Johnson, the famous woman pilot, flew in. Poor Daddy was sorely disappointed as "the de Havilland Rapide in which we circled the tower had only small porthole-like windows and I was too small to see out of them".

He went on to Leigh Grammar School when he was ten where he made good friends, including Jimmy Heath. The two of them used to go on long cycle rides out along the canals past industrial mills and warehouses both to get to school and at weekends onwards out into the countryside. I can remember him telling me that once they bumped into a tramp who was living in a hedge who took one look at them and told them to "shove off". Once they found a fisherman's dinghy hidden in the long grass along the canal. They launched in the water and Jimmy jumped aboard but it was quickly swept away and there was no means of steering. Daddy describes following it helplessly for a mile or so until a man grabbed the rope and hauled it to shore. There were many unemployed men then who used to spend the day in the fields with their dogs and it was one of these men who rescued Jimmy.

Meanwhile my mother was growing up in London, her father working at Great Ormond Street. Here's a studio photo showing Mummy with her younger sister, Janet.

A studio photo of Valerie and Janet Bentler

A FAMILY TREE

I don't know where they first lived but when she was nine war broke out and her parents decided that the children had to leave central London. While her parents were looking for a house I believe that she and her sister, Janet, went to their Aunt Rhoda, in Yorkshire, which was not, for whatever reason, a happy time as I've explained earlier. But they soon all moved to a bungalow by the River Thames at Bourne End, which Mummy loved. I remember her saying what a long journey she had to school but how much she enjoyed it. First they had to row across the river, then walk to the bus stop and catch the bus into Maidenhead. Mummy always loved the water and later took every opportunity to go sailing with Pat and Dennis Guest, who were my parents' great friends in Bolton. Mummy had mastoids when she was little and was not allowed to go swimming lest she got an ear infection. I also always understood that she had had the less serious version of meningitis and had to lie in a dark room for a long time while she recovered. Of course, my grandparents will have been extremely anxious given what had happened to Granny's sister, Marguerite.

I knew how much Mummy liked the river and when she died, Daddy and I decided to spread her ashes near the bungalow she'd lived in during the war at Bourne End. I could see how much fun it must have been to live there. Opposite us on the other bank of the Thames stands a line of bungalows looking out over the river. Theirs was the last with no more than a footpath between the house and the bank and fields both to the side and at the back. It must have been good fun in contrast to central London. Grandpa had to commute but out in the country all was calm. I realise that he had a very long journey as he had already started his job as the medical superintendent of Highwood Hospital in Brentwood, Essex, specialising in TB in children. Maybe he only came home at the weekend. I remember Granny saying that their relationship did go into a period of great strain during this time and Mummy recalled terrible arguments but I know she enjoyed living there. She was a girl who loved climbing trees and messing about in boats. When my parents bought our house, Raihaan, in Kenley, Surrey, when I was nine, she particularly hoped that Mark and I would love climbing the trees at the bottom of the garden where there was a regular wood and a very big climbable beech tree. Although we did play down there, we never spent as much time climbing as she clearly would have done if she'd had that garden, so I know we were a bit of a disappointment.

Daddy was 11 when the war started. He remembers the day war broke out. The vicar was in the middle of his sermon in church when a man advanced towards him down the central aisle holding a piece of paper. *"The vicar read what was in the paper, fell silent for a moment and then said that the prime minister had just announced over the radio that Hitler had ignored our ultimatum to stop his invasion of Poland and Britain was therefore at war with Germany. Again silence and the vicar broke into prayer. Three or four young women burst into tears. I remember thinking that we were unlikely to win the war if that was the reaction"*. That night they had hardly gone to sleep when the air raid warning siren sounded. They hurried across the main road to great-aunt Maud's house where they went down into the cellar. They sat there for 20 minutes while great-uncle Rupert nailed a cloth over the cellar's barred window and wet it as a precaution against gas. *"Then Aunt Maud announced she intended to make us a cup of tea which involved going up into the kitchen. I thought she was very brave considering the danger we were all in. The tea arrived and we had hardly drunk any when the siren sounded 'all clear'. I felt let down as it proved to have been a false raid alarm due to a British aircraft being misidentified as a German"*.

In Leigh things were mostly calm but they had to carry their gas masks at all times and they did so for several years and had regular drills at school. He says how very unpleasant the masks were to wear as they were made of heavy rubber, hot, smelly and very hard to breathe through. Granny and great-aunt Frances volunteered at the air raid warning centre. The job was to operate the radio and if word of an air raid came in then the phone operator had to start the siren to warn everyone to go down to into the bomb shelters. I don't think they usually had much to do and no doubt a fair amount of chat went on. I like to think of them sitting there with their head phones part on part off. But there were some planes which flew over after bombing Liverpool with the odd stray bomb left to drop. On one famous evening, Granny was in charge of the headset and got a signal but was in such a state of shock she fainted and no one knew what she'd been told. My father used to tell this story with great glee and get engulfed in gasps of laughter as he told it.

Anyone who ever heard my father tell a story knew how likely he was to choke on his own laughter and then not be able to complete the story. This would always set everyone off and before long we were all shaking with laughter too. Many years later, when Kate and Ben were six months old, we all went to spend Christmas in Honfleur in Normandy (Alex, me and Kate, Mark, Bunky and Ben, my parents and Margit). A certain amount of Calvados used to be had in the evening and somehow each day it seemed to be someone else's turn to have too much. One evening, my mother laughed so much she fell off her chair and disappeared under the table, not her normal behaviour. Another evening, my father went to the toilet and when he'd been gone for some time I got worried and went to see what had happened and to my horror I heard loud groaning from the other side of the door. I was convinced he was having a heart attack and cried out but he pulled himself together and explained that he was just laughing having remembered some funny story he was telling earlier on. This is how "have another Calvados" became a family expression.

When Daddy was 13 he was sent off to boarding school. His mother chose Worksop, a school which looks quite nice now but then was a gloomy old place with cold showers and dormitories. My father was resentful when his mother later explained that he could have gone to Winchester but Worksop seemed more convenient. Later, when Daddy got into New College at Oxford, a large proportion of the students had been to Winchester and tended not even to have heard of Worksop. But Daddy had some good stories. The food was obviously terrible. They used to have "chocolate pudding" which had nothing to do with chocolate and they were convinced was made of mud. The teaching was not much good either and they had one history teacher who used to fall asleep during the lessons. One day the entire class moved their desks behind him so that when the bell rang and he woke up with a start there were no boys and no desks in front of him. And Daddy also made two of his very best friends, Bob Scrivins and Peter Roberts. Bob Scrivins had many important roles in my father's life: he was best man at my parents' wedding, my godfather, and was also married to Jean who much later became my stepmother after my mother died. The three of them went on a motorbike ride over the Alps to Italy after school and obviously had great fun including earning free beers in bars by singing silly songs.

Meanwhile, Mummy's family moved back into London. I'm not clear about the dates but both Bentley girls went to Henrietta Barnett Secondary School so they must have moved back into London during the war. They lived not far from the school in Hampstead Garden Suburb at no. 1 Green Tiles. There are a lot of very smart houses round the corner (Bishop's Avenue being a highly "favoured" address), but the Bentleys lived in a semi-detached on the main road, the A1. We've driven past it often. It has a green roof and is at the end of the row of houses overlooking the main road, a big contrast from the bungalow on the Thames.

Mummy also made some of her best lifelong friends at Henrietta Barnett School, in particular Helen and Angela. They were a real gang. Helen married a Dutch man called Hans Moller and became my godmother. Meanwhile Angela completely astonished the group when, on the morning of their first A-level exam, she came in wearing an engagement ring. Her fiancé was Derek Taunt, a man 17 years older than her, and everyone was so excited they couldn't concentrate on the exam. Derek became the treasurer of a Cambridge College and they had a nice house overlooking Parker's Piece. The house was full of paintings by Ben Nicholson, one of England's most famous 20th century artists. Angela was an artist herself and in her 40s got a job working for Ben as his assistant, going on tour with him to Italy. He'd given her several paintings. Of course, as a child this meant nothing to me and all I can really remember is that we were staying with them in 1966 when England won the World Cup against Germany. I remember us all sitting round the TV watching the football when my tooth came out as England got its final winning goal and no one was remotely impressed by my tooth.

A FAMILY TREE

What brought my parents together was their love of history which they both studied at Oxford. My father first had to do his military service which was then obligatory. I never got the impression that he'd enjoyed it. Hard to imagine but he was a boxer and had his two front teeth knocked out in a boxing match while in the army and had to have false teeth (his teeth were very poor and he landed up having them all removed). We as children used to love trying to get him to take his dentures out which he never did until once at a party in the kitchen he started to laugh so much that his teeth went one way and he fell the other. I was in the kitchen as a teenager and remember feeling both gripped and appalled.

Mummy went to work as an au pair in Paris and spent a good deal of time with her cousin, Dennis, and, I assume, his Parisian wife. She also made life-long friends with Elisabeth Hainoux, whose granddaughter did a rather ill-fated French exchange with our daughter, Harriet, many decades later. She obviously learned excellent French while there and I recall being frustrated at being told how very good her French was when we were living in Provence and my parents came to visit for Christmas.

Daddy's French was never any good but at some point he went on an English-Speaking Union trip to Provence with a group of fellow students where he had a marvellous time including gate-crashing an event which De Gaulle was speaking at when he had announced that he refused to have anyone British present. My father was so incensed that somehow he blagged his way in (heaven knows how, given his accent) and managed to stand in line to shake de Gaulle's hand at the end, much to the future president of France's great irritation.

As a result of his stint in the army and, maybe her time as an au pair, they both started at university at the same time. Daddy at New College with all the posh Winchester boys who he always felt uncomfortable with and Mummy at St Anne's, which was not yet a university college but she was allowed to take a degree – one of the few women there. Neither of them ever said much about their time there. When I went to Oxford and asked Mummy what it was like in her day, she said, 'I don't remember, I think I was drunk at the time.' And certainly for a very clever person, it's striking that she only got a third. Meanwhile my father only ever gave the impression that it was hard having a Northern accent and only having been at a very minor public school compared with the grandeur of the Winchester boys. I think he liked his studies and certainly some fun was had. He once managed, with an enthusiastic sweeping hand gesture, to tear down a wire which fused all the lights in the Taj Mahal restaurant in Turl Street. But apart from that I heard very little about their respective times. My father was viva'd for a first. The examiner said that he had clearly known nothing at all about Simon De Montfort in the exam essay he wrote on the topic and asked what he knew now. The answer was still nothing so he landed up with a second.

They met at Oxford but didn't fall for each other at the time. At some point she had an Italian boyfriend who she was keen on until she went to stay with his family in Italy and saw a rather different person to her romantic ideal. At university my mother was keen on a New Zealander called Don Beulay (who was also a friend of my father's) but after university he broke it off. She got a job working in Manchester as a secretary and it was Don who encouraged my father, who was then working for the *Leigh Journal* (back in his home town) not far away, to get in touch with Valerie. He told me that he took her out for a drink and was very taken aback when she asked for a whisky and not a Babycham (a substitute champagne-type drink served in a flat glass always with a picture of a Bambi-type baby deer enjoying the bubbles) which he thought would have been much more ladylike, and probably cheaper too. She was getting over Don Beulay's rejection and Daddy had recently split up with a French girl who he'd been to visit in Calais who he decided was very nice but not a *wife*. Obviously they hit it off and got married just over a year later.

But in the meantime there were decisions to be made about my father's career. He had started as a junior journalist with the *Leigh Journal* and recalled turning up to his first assignment without either pencil or notepad. He really wanted to join the Foreign Office but after failing the exam it was GB who put him in touch with an old boy of hers who was working for the

Daily Telegraph. He got a job there and Mummy moved back down South to work as a PA at the BBC. She worked on the Fanny Craddock cookery show. Fanny was Britain's first TV chef and a real battle-axe of a woman who mercilessly bossed her (fourth) husband, "Major Johnnie", around in the stage kitchen but not nearly as bossily as she treated my mother and the supporting team. She had a reputation for a scathing tongue but it may well be that she did teach Mummy a good deal about cooking. She had a reputation for having brought French and Italian cuisine to England and for having popularised the pizza before it had been taken on by the English. Certainly, Mummy was a very good cook and introduced us to many delicious and, in those days, new tastes. A double page article appeared in the *Bolton Evening News* featuring Mark and me, aged two and four enjoying her "exotic" cooking: pasta, curry and chop suey. She taught me what she regarded as the basics: how to make a white sauce and those three dishes as staples beyond which you could then develop your own ideas. In the days before recipe books became popular (and certainly nothing available online) she always used to cut recipes out of the newspaper and stick them in a scrapbook which she kept in the kitchen. It was well used and revealed the oil and flours and spices which had been used around it.

At the *Telegraph* my father was given the chance to be the acting editor for a couple of weeks. It wasn't my father's politics to write for, or even read, the *Telegraph* and this difference showed up very clearly when the first big news story broke. London had always suffered from bad fogs ("pea-soupers") but in 1952 what became known as the "Great Smog" lasted 4 days, killing an estimated 4,000 people and making 100,000 very ill. My father's view was that this was a national crisis and that Churchill was mismanaging it so he wrote a critical editorial. The editor came down on him like a ton of bricks and said the *Telegraph* does *not* criticise the prime minister and told him to go away and rewrite it. When a couple of days later, a national crisis was declared and Churchill changed his stance, the editor was even less pleased with my father. That seemed to mark the beginning of the end of his high aspirations for promotion.

I've found a diary Daddy kept at the time. It starts on 26th August 1954 when he was living at the Central YMCA in Great Russell Street and is headed "A failure starting upwards...". He had just been told by the *Daily Telegraph* that he would not work as a leader again. *"My mood was a sickening mixture of numbness and hysteria... my last leader, as with all the others, had been shredded and rehashed"*. The diary goes on with a great deal of self-doubt and uncertainty as to what he would do next. He seemed to go to the cinema every day, see quite a few friends but then went on to criticise them. In fact, the *Telegraph* gave him a job as a sub-editor and sent him off to Bonn, then the capital city of Germany.

At some point, but it's not clear when, he proposed and they agreed to get married and so the long distance correspondence started. Mummy was in London living at 65 Egerton Gardens, SW1, with Helen. The two of them wrote to one another incredibly frequently. Among my parents' papers there are literally hundreds of letters which they seemed to write nearly every single day. They both comment on how quickly the post travelled so if either missed a day, one (usually my mother) would moan that clearly the other didn't love them enough and must have gone off with someone more exciting. She writes complaining that she has to go to work in despair yet again, due to another day without a letter. He writes back to point out that he does have a busy new job and that he has to write articles for the next day's paper until late at night. They spend a lot of time questioning "what is love?" and do they really care, etc., etc.

The fact is that his letters are at their most interesting when he's writing about news events in Germany. For instance, after I was born, he wrote to his mother about going to see Churchill's visit to the 4th Hussars in Northern Germany. *"My first viewing of the old man. Old he certainly is, uncertain on his feet, rather glassy-eyed and easily tired. His voice is still clear and firm though... Old or no his speech was pungent enough to excite the politicians here. His proposal is to bring Russia 'if reformed' into NATO – really upset Adenauer (Germany's Chancellor) who sat with a stunned face during the speech and, unusually for him, stuttered over his own address.*

The repercussions are still being felt". He goes on to write about him and Mummy visiting Belsen concentration camp which is next door to the Hussars' barracks. "*Nothing is left now except long, low piles of heather covered earth marking the mass graves and a few memorials erected by Jewish relatives of the dead and a large monolith backed by a stone wall with inscriptions in several languages. Nature is kind in obliterating these horrible places but it is rather dreadful to think how soon the victims are forgotten*". He also writes very interestingly about the complexity of German recognition (or not) of what had happened during the war. At this point, the government and Adenauer were involved in a process of forgetting and it was some years before the truth was faced. I remember Daddy telling us about visiting the hotel where Hitler came to oversee the murder of his old party comrade, Roehm, and his supporters on what became known as the Night of the Long Knives, in 1934. One of the people my father interviewed was the lady who owned the hotel who was still talking about what a very nice and polite man Hitler had been, no trouble at all!

It's clear from my parents' letters to each other that in many ways they didn't know one another very well and they were both nervous and had rather cinematic ideas of what romance was all about. But it's also clear that they really did love each other.

But all was not well with the families on either side. Mary was unhappy in love and in life generally and, perhaps inevitably, relations with her were always strained. I'm not sure about Granny but I doubt that she and Mummy ever had a good relationship. Meanwhile the Bentleys never approved of their son-in-law and it is clear from the letters that once when he went to Brentwood to visit her parents, they seem to have had the most terrible row after Frank and Jo had been "most uncivil" and criticised the *Daily Telegraph* for their politics, which he also disagreed with, but he certainly didn't appreciate his prospective parents-in-law having a go at him. The animosity never went away and I was very aware of it as a child.

The fact is that they both came from very different backgrounds but were not yet at ease in mixing across class and background. Daddy came from a professional university background, as did Mummy, and neither were posh. But the Bentleys no doubt had a feeling of superiority to the Lancashire lot with their Lancastrian accents and the mining town they lived in, whilst also feeling the pinch that it was Granny Hope who had inherited wealth while they were striving, first generation immigrants. And, on the other hand, Lancashire most likely had never known anyone from Hungary or Russia or with Jewish backgrounds and probably felt rather uncomfortable with them both because they were "other" but also because they were Londoners and more urbane. None of this was ever voiced, or even thought of to my knowledge, but it strained all relations.

My parents were a product of their generation. They were educated and liberal-minded. But they had closed ideas about the life they were meant to lead. The man was meant to go to work and have a profession. My father was a journalist and his parents-in-law thought him brash, noisy and not well-heeled. The wife was meant to cook and clean and make the home nice, which my mother did but as a result she never had the chance to even start to meet her potential. She later became a history teacher and was good at it but it wasn't her vocation, more something that was convenient with her school holidays coinciding with ours as children. Her mother-in-law and sister-in-law, who did not work, will have been aware of her frustrations and thereby the innate criticism of their own job-free lives. My father never earned much money and the need to make savings was always apparent. They certainly weren't poor in any way but normal life involved no luxuries. We only ever went on camping holidays, hotels were out of the question, we only ate meat once a week, we never ate out in a restaurant, my father had one bottle of beer on Wednesday and another on Saturday, wine was not bought, and, apart from Mrs Partington for a few years in Bolton, Mummy had no help in the house. Things did change when my father inherited money after his mother and sister died but that was well after I'd grown up and left home. They were never at ease with anyone who was wealthier and more travelled than them.

The strain with the Bentley parents shows up in their letters planning the wedding, all of which they had to do long-distance. Mummy's young sister, Janet, had also got engaged to Lawrence Miller, a local accountant from a long-standing Brentwood Essex family. How it happened I don't know but Janet and Lawrence had their wedding two weeks before my parents and then couldn't come to the wedding as they were still on honeymoon. The younger sister got married from the family home while my parents were married in London and the letters reveal some fuss over where the reception could be held. Janet's wedding took place on 27th August 1955 and my parents on 10th September 1955.

Daddy wrote from Bonn after Janet's wedding, *"I fell more in love with you last weekend than ever before. My heart couldn't be more full... you are my life, my love, my all. Never were you more lovely than in that picture hat, smiling and radiant. The dress was beautiful. Far more important though you were so gracious and charming. Darling, darling, darling Valerie... No man could deserve such a wife as you shall be... When I say those wedding vows I know I shall mean them more than anything else I've said in my life... It seems 14 years and not 14 months since we met under the portico of Manchester library. Then you had that awful sack of a coat and I looked like something out of a detective novel"*.

I have no similar description of how they felt about their own wedding but they look very happy in the photographs. It must have been a big thing to go off to Germany. For Mummy it involved giving up her job, leaving her friends and moving to a country she didn't know and a language she didn't speak. But more than anything she wanted to be married and my sense is that they loved creating their own life away from the awkwardness of relations with their respective in-laws. Did they talk about her Jewish background, his Lancashire family, of the Ronas having to escape Hungary in the same year I was born? Or were they just intent on creating their own family?

My parents leave their wedding on 12th September 1956

And so we leave my parents getting into the wedding car and going off on their honeymoon to Italy before moving to Bonn, where I was born just over nine months later on 16 July 1956.

Plate from the hospital in Bonn where I was born at 8.24pm on 16th July 1956

The hospital presented my parents with this plate showing the time and date of my birth. And so Diana Frances Hope arrives in post-war Germany carrying the DNA and experiences of all the people I've described in here but with her own life ahead of her. Exciting.

7. Chronology

I think it's fascinating to go back and create a chronology of the critical dates for the people in the family I've been writing about. There are so many overlaps. From this I can see that both my Russian and Hungarian great-grandfathers died in the same year, 1929 – the year after my father was born; that my two grandfathers were nearly at Durham University at the same time; that my father was born in the year in which his parents-in-law-to-be (the Bentleys) got married; and that 1930 was the year when my mother was born, as was my father's sister, Mary, and that that was also the year that my father's father also died; that my grandmother's cousins, the Ronas, escaped Hungary in the same year I was born, 1956. All these events coinciding years before anyone knew that there would be a link.

1847:   William Prescott (Lancashire great-grandfather born)

1852 or 1854: Hyman Benjamin (Russian great-grandfather born)

1855:   Frances Chadwick born (Lancashire great-grandmother born)

1867:   Double wedding of Adolf Reichenfeld and Rozalia Grosz together with Roza Grosz and Moritz Reichenfeld

1874:   Hyman Benjamin marries first wife, Rachel Tuchman

1891:   Joseph Whittle Hope (Lancashire grandfather) born in Leigh, Lancashire

1893:   Sarah Evelyne Prescott (Lancashire grandmother) born in Leigh, Lancashire

1899:   Francis Joseph Benjamin (Bentley) (Russian grandfather) born 28/12/1899 in Middlesborough

A FAMILY TREE

	(but note records show: January 1900 per Civil Registration Birth Index and the 1901 Census has him as aged 1)
1903:	Josephine Lily Richfield (Hungarian grandmother) born 24/1/1903 in Bristol
1914:	William Prescott dies in April 1914
1914:	WWI starts on 28 July 1914
1916:	Joseph Hope ordained deacon and priest in 1916 at Durham University
1917:	Joseph Hope sent to the front in France on 18/12/1917
1918:	Frank Benjamin (Bentley) starts at Durham University in October 1918
1918:	WWI ends on 11/11/1918
1919:	Dennis Bloodworth born London 24/5/1919
1920:	Joseph Hope and Sarah Evelyne Prescott marry at Leigh Parish Church on 21/10/1920
1921:	Arthur Hope (first son of Lancashire grandparents) born and dies
1922:	Frank Benjamin (Bentley) graduates as a doctor from Durham University
1928:	Michael Hope born on 21/1/1928 at Woodplumpton, Lancashire
1928:	Jo Richfield and Frank Benjamin get married
1929:	Hyman Benjamin (Russian great-grandfather) dies in Middlesbrough; and Adolf Reichenfeld (Hungarian great-grandfather) dies in Hungary.
1929:	Bentleys change name from Benjamin to Bentley
1930:	Frances Mary Hope born on 3/2/1930

CHRONOLOGY

1930:	Valerie Bentley born on 18/5/1930
1930:	Joseph Hope dies on 26/10/1930 of appendicitis
1932:	Janet Bentley born
1939:	July 1939 Frances Prescott (née Chadwick, my Lancashire granny's mother dies)
1939:	Bentley grandparents visit Laci and Judy Rona in Budapest
1939:	WWII starts on 1/8/1939
1944:	Judy sent to Auschwitz in November 1944
1945:	Judy leaves first Auschwitz and then Boizenburg and returns to Budapest
1945:	8/5/1945 WWII ends in Europe
1955:	Valerie Bentley and Michael Hope get married
1955:	Dennis Bloodworth and Ching Ping meet and marry in Hong Kong
1956:	Diana Hope born on 16 July 1956
1956:	Hungary Uprising and Ronas escape to England
1958:	Mark Hope born on 17 October 1958
1967:	Frank Bentley dies at Hurlingham Club on 10/9/1967
1980:	Sarah Evelyne Hope dies on 29 January 1980
1991:	Jo Bentley dies on 17/5/1991
1993:	Mary Hope dies aged 63
2003:	Valerie Hope dies in the night after her 73rd birthday on 19/5/2003
2005:	Dennis Bloodworth dies in Singapore
2020:	Michael Hope dies aged 92 on 16/9/2020

8. Appendices

Appendix 1: The Journal (written by a friend of Judy Rona's and translated by Judy's daughter Mary about their journey from Boizenburg camp back to Budapest in 1945. Judy is referred to in the journal by her original Hungarian name, Jutka.)

28 April 1945. Boizenburg lager (camp) Evening Appel (roll call) in the yard. The old Kommandant gathered us round him in a semi-circle, saying he had an announcement to make. Lina, the number one beast, stood next to him, wearing coarse grey trousers. She was in a good mood and this misled us.

We haven't gone to work in the factory for days, they have kept us busy with various jobs they've found for us to do; the weather is good and it's better not to dwell on the thought that lilacs are beginning to blossom but we are still here. For days now we've been going to sleep having been told that we might be setting out on a journey at dawn – everybody should make a bundle of their bits and pieces – I don't know what from, but we're supposed to do it. And if we don't go, we can carry on listening to the aerial bombardments.

We'd like to have these preparations behind us, we listen to the latest announcement with indifference, but this seems more serious; they give us bread, beetroot, tinned meat, margarine, of course only a small portion of everything, not to overburden our digestion, we have to admit they are taking care of us, looking after our wellbeing. So we're off at dawn. We've to clean everything thoroughly. We don't sleep much, we want to have a wash as well, who knows when we'll be able to get water again. At dawn Appel, line-up.

We set off, armed with our bundles. First we are lined up in fours, then later in twos; we march and march. My partner is Ila, in front of me and behind me go Margit with Gitta, Jutka with Panni, Klari, Anci, Ilonka. We're in a good mood, there's something in the air, perhaps liberation. Nobody can tell us anything. The whole camp and hospital are on the move with us. They drive us on frequently as we go, we fall behind a bit. If we can't take the pace, we get a blow on the back. We mutter something between our teeth, we can't complain aloud. Little Trude, the tamest aufseherin (supervisor) has turned wild. Big Trude made off long ago. We're passing through beautiful countryside with lilacs everywhere; people stare at us from their gardens as if we were some sort of wonder. We see chickens and pigs. It's warm.

We have walked and walked, we have got very tired. At last we are allowed to rest. We are in a village, the brutes find shelter for us, after a lot of looking round we are allowed up into a hayloft, it's a good place, we have to go up big ladders to get there, my bandaged leg isn't even hurting, but I'm scared of straining it, on the other hand I don't want to fall behind. So we settle down for the night, but before that the owner lets us cook some of the semolina he has given us, Ilonka and Sari cook, I carry it up the ladder, I climb up a few more times, I do what I need to, it's suspicious that there are discarded weapons everywhere, as if there's something wrong perhaps? Our aufseher has been harsh to us on our way just as before, looking at us with disgust, in other words nothing has changed. We note this and lie down. In the morning it's up and carry on, we walk and walk and walk. It's evening, our second place of rest is an awful stable, some dirty Ukrainians were here before us, we're worried we might catch something from them.

We set off again early in the morning, it's cold, the sun has gone in, but the bombs keep falling, we're far from Boizenburg now, we can see from the road signs. In one of our stopping places no one wanted to give us any shelter, so they left us to stand in the street with hail falling on us, we huddled together, our blanket, just a small piece of rag, is soaking wet, we are shivering. What will become of us? Stables, barns, no proper place to wash anywhere. We'd like to be able to speak to someone who knows something.

Our route takes us through beautiful woods, in different circumstances we could even enjoy seeing them, bombed out tanks, vehicles everywhere. They're taking us a roundabout way, not to meet the enemy head on, till at last on the fourth day Margit says they can't be far and so asked a passing woman, a civilian, where is the enemy, to which she answered half an hour from here. Next we came to a crossroads, two striking looking Americans on motorbikes stopped us with a friendly smile, asked to see the papers of the leaders and then they let us proceed, we didn't understand what was going on, are we free? Yes. You could hear people all over the place saying that they were just taking us on to Neustadt, to a lager, as instructed. After that we naturally walked with a lighter step, the SS women had disappointed looks on their faces and also they got changed with civilian clothes under their collars, what happened was that we rested in a wood while they got down in a bunker.

We got to Neustadt. We could see already from a distance that something was burning. It must be the lager, where Ukrainian women were making a commotion, starting fires. They threw out loaves of bread, items of clothing on to the street, of course we didn't get any of it. Things didn't look too promising, the rain started coming down, the whole caravan was crying, the Kommandant made a speech in the pouring rain, nobody should lose their head, he'll take us back to where there are Americans and hand us over, only we should behave ourselves. We promised everything, we just wanted to go. One of the harsh Schaaarfuhrers took little Fulecske on his back, saying she's got a weak heart, she can't walk.

When we got to a bridge, the other one, the chief Kommandant, took off his bayonet, broke it on the railing of the bridge and hurled it far away. The others followed suit with their weapons. It was good to see. Amidst discarded weapons, backpacks, blouses, shirts, we reached the Americans stationed in the village, they offered us cigarettes, reassured us, everybody should go where they could find a place for themselves, they would take care of us in the morning. This was a setback for our hopes, we had imagined ourselves in hotels, in beds. Too bad, it doesn't matter. Another hay shed, but they did offer us milk and bread. The straw was cold and our resting place hard, but we are no longer Haftlinge (prisoners) and that warms us up.

Morning has come, it's time to get up, but no longer at anyone's command. It's a nice sunny May morning, flowers, people, and we can go about freely. Our fellow women emerge from the houses, the smarter ones have had milk, got hold of bread, by the time we set off to get something to eat there's nothing to be had. We lady knights decorated with the star. The owner of our house takes pity on us and gives everyone a bit of milk, we line up for a joke, we set off and sing as we make for our destination, we pass through woods, pleasant little settlements on our way to Ludviglust, our stopping place. We get there after four days' march.

These are the scenes that followed: large crowds in the street, they are Germans staring, then the Jews, not just ours, but Haftlinge, men and women brought here from all parts of the country assail the Germans, tear off their necklaces, watches, bicycles and took everything they found on them. the astonished crowd just stood and stared. This is a beautiful little town, with a hotel, a hairdresser, and every kind of culture we have not seen for a very long time. It would be really good to have a perm done, I think to myself, but it remains only a thought as we carry on, afraid of missing any transport that might be going.

We imagined they would put us straightaway on a luxurious train and take us home. It's just a matter of time, I console myself, because we're going home, but when? Soon. Before they take us to our lodgings they sit us down in a big square where American soldiers are taking photographs, the smarter ones come by tins of food, cigarettes. As for us, we sit like elegant ladies, thinking they'll bring us something on a gold tray. We were wrong. Even our clever Gitta is sitting here with us, while dear Margit is wondering what we could do, by the time we've thought it out it's time to go. In the meantime, llonka and I knock on a house to use their facilities, they don't open the door, we're already on our way, but they run after us, what do we want, we tell them, come in, stay with us, they say, they offer us ham and potatoes, but there's no time to eat it, we'll get left behind, we run carrying the red pot, offer some to everyone, it's so long since we had decent food, and this really was decent food. Well at last after a short walk, we arrived in a garden suburb, the Finns are already killing each other for a good place to stay, we're waiting around as usual, by the time we get in everything has been looted, prized open, what's more within 10 minutes they had taken away the keys to the larder from some departing Germans amidst death threats, we look on with disgust and starve. At last we found a place on the ground floor, then upstairs. It's a nice room, we needed to fight a bit for it and by some miracle we actually did. There are mattresses here and pillows, blankets we already have. We find some blackberry juice, tinned food, cigars, flour, sugar. Magda Weiss, Mrs. Bibor and Mrs. Fischer with her daughter Magda stay with us for a few days, we cook a nice goulash with potatoes together. Unfortunately I can't eat any of it, I don't feel well, we find groats as well, groats in water, we stuff them into stoves, that is to say we cook in them, I kneel a lot, and this makes my leg hurt, but we are free and that makes my situation easier. In the evening we sleep with the window open, there is no need for blackout, can that be true?

Today there was a séance round the table. Magda Wesz got very bad news, we had a very sad evening. Zsuzsa Hevesi, our English interpreter says we could soon be leaving. This morning our Kommandant was partying with the tipsy Schaarfuhrer, we found some wine, we gave them some, we even offered them cigars. Our Lageralteste visited us with her entourage, everything is going very well, chicken paprikas from the American kitchen, and everything is fine. She looks very well, elegant, surrounded by secretaries, and so she gives us only promises. Everyone is looking after their own affairs now, as she says, she is nothing to do with us, and she shows it. Marcsa has come to visit us as well, splendid clothes, shoes, our rags are nothing short of disgraceful, so I chase the young ones out into the street, I can see everyone is carrying baggage, clothing, food, go and get something. But they didn't come back, they were seized and taken somewhere, no one knows where. I've made a nice lunch and only we, the middle aged ones, eat it. Towards midday a messenger comes: the Americans have seized everyone on the streets, and driven them into some barracks, and from there no one knows where to. Ilonka is packing, disconsolate, so is Mrs. Fischer, we too are getting ready, when the prisoners appear and say everyone on the streets had their papers checked, because the Jews were taking their looting too far.

If this is right, I'm never giving advice again, I'm not cut out to be a Mrs. Warren. They've brought a lot of SS coats with them and they couldn't tell us enough about their adventure, what happened, how it happened, what they got, they flirted, there were lots of French, everyone had their own success story. I was longing for trousers, they didn't bring any, I hope we can get hold of one single pair of trousers later. There's a rumour that we are going to set off again, but there are no trucks yet. I am excited, up to now my leg hasn't been hurting, but now it's hurting a lot, it looks as if there's no end to this, I would like to avoid being a burden on anyone, to drift away from the group, but Ilonka is always looking for me and it's impossible to escape. I keep wandering about, jumping up and down, when I ought to be resting, we're not setting off, only tomorrow. The weather is nice. There isn't enough room for us, so Margit, who doesn't allow herself to be put off by anyone, goes in search of new accommodation, she's right. She finds a place in a beautiful villa on the opposite side of the road, a nice room, there are several people living in the place, there's a bathroom as well. It's civilised here, there just isn't anything for us to eat. Maggi soup again. Dear Margit is tireless in her search. She succeeds in finding some useful things, but not food, unfortunately. I don't feel well, my leg hurts a lot. We ask the doctor, a German. He says we're leaving any way, there will be a doctor at our next stopping place, I should get myself seen there. We're all in bad shape.

Liberation, eagerly awaited as it was, has caught us a little unprepared. We do actually set off the next day, we only slept one night in genteel comfort.

We pack and meet up. Gitta has fallen out with us because I told her off a bit after Parni complained about her, I'm afraid, so she's not coming with us, so for the first time someone has left our group. It's upsetting, but she won't work together with the rest of the group. Some trucks have come, we clamber on and we're off, there's no knowing where our next stopping place will be.

A FAMILY TREE

Our vehicle takes us through the main square of the town, where the dead bodies of men lie covered on the ground, they're burying them as well as the Jewish men who have died here of starvation. This produced a terrible effect on us. Everyone thought of their own man, but was afraid to say anything. The way we're going is beautiful, at last we stop. Enormous hangars, they're really lagers, it's like the tower of Babel, so many languages, prisoners of so many nationalities, waiting to be disinfected, this consisted of the American soldiers spraying our heads and arms with powder, apparently this is more effective than disinfecting people naked. From here we elbow our way into some officers' quarters in the same area, it's very hard to get a place, others are better at pushing their way in, so they're already in there. Klari is the vanguard, Margit, Ila and I after her, the others find a place in a different building, there are beds in our room, with blankets on them, so we can leave our rags behind. Before settling down I spoke to some men from the Hungarian forced labour service, their faces, their hands dreadfully beaten up. Men of 80 kilos reduced to 35 kilos and they say everyone who didn't die looks like this. I've got a terrible pain in my heart, my stomach, I feel I'm not going to make it, but now when we are getting near to home? I can't walk any more, I feel sick, I've got a high temperature, diarrhea, I can't get up or go out. Margit, Ila and Ilonka are frightened, don't say goodbye to me yet, I say, I want to live some more yet. They bring buckets, they don't let me go out, I have no strength at all. They're all working instead of me, they don't let me get up, the Hungarian doctor comes, he examines me, I'm a suspected case of typhus. My temperature is 41C. What will become of me, you can go, leave me here, I'll follow you, I say, I don't want to be a burden to you, I can't stand the thought of anyone being put out because of me. But they don't take the slightest notice of me. They keep bringing lovely food, I can't eat any, American ham, soups with bacon, lots of it, but I can't eat a thing, that's another tragedy. If I were well, I would eat the lot, I say, I wouldn't leave you anything. Ionka has been out about eighty-six times to fetch something I would eat and I don't feel like anything. Dear Margit manages to get some tea, drink that, it's nice. The weather is beautiful, it would be nice to go out, and I'm going to, supported on each side I could go to the American medical station. And that is what we do, dear Margit and Klari come with me, I feel practically as if I've been born again, the fever's gone, I'm in great pain, but I don't say anything, I don't want to frighten them, I've given everyone quite enough trouble already. Margit is also not well, she's in bed for a day, but she's strong, while I've become a sickly sort. Well, I suppose I'll get better sooner or later. There's a rumour that they're transferring us to the Russians, we don't mind, so long as we get going somewhere. At one o'clock midday one fine day the jeeps make their appearance, we get on and go. I can't see Gitta, I don't know where she is, the unfaithful dog. After travelling for half an hour we arrive in Grabow. Russian occupation, we saw Russian guards before as well. So we've progressed by one staging post. We get off, everyone goes where they can find a place, they don't give us any directions, some people have found somewhere already by the time we march into a cinema. Urania. It looks as if it was nice once, now it's dirty, strewn with straw, smelly, everything's broken, but there's a piano, and boxes and stalls as well, we make ourselves comfortable. Magda Weiss plays the piano amongst the broken lights and glasses. We meet some of our mates, they're well dressed already. We have to look for accommodation and we have found a room in the inn next door. We've never seen such filth, feathers, straw, broken crocks, awful smell everywhere. Not a bit of food anywhere.

It's not a good place, we go to the Conditorei. There we settled down in the red salon, on the floor of course. They're not looking after us, in the courtyard some Russians are cooking, the trick is to catch the right time, when? Jutka and I stand at the window, they chase us away, we clear off. Some people are smarter and manage to get something to eat. At last they give us some rubbishy soup out of pity. We'd really like to eat our fill of decent food for once. There are washing facilities and in a neighbouring garden some maggi soup is cooking on two bricks for our lot. I'm bored with it. The Finns are making chremsel, one of them offers me some, I'm scared to accept it, who knows what she's put into it. But I still bite into it, then I run to the back. It's warm day and night, as usual I can't sleep. Margit invites me for a walk. We have a look at the bar, we are sad to see the beautiful fittings broken. My leg is hurting a lot and I'm itching a lot by now from vitamin deficiency. In the morning go to the Russian medical station, just then a chambermaid is sitting on the doctor's lap. He has no time to see to me. So I go to the Hungarian hospital, with a few friends, Ilonka and Klari among them. They receive us with great hostility. They're brimming with hatred. Now, now, doctor, you little fascist, none of it's our fault, yes it is, says one of the doctors, we, or some of our women, said they were Szalasi's soldiers, we think to ourselves. Are they going to give us treatment or not, we have come here, where there are Hungarians, all excited, and this is how they deal with us.

We leave and take note. Then another doctor came who was kinder and ushered us into the ward, where they bandage me up and give us the medication we need as far as possible. The way back is very nice. We decide that we are going to loot, that's all very well, but there's nothing to loot.

All the shops are empty. Back in our digs Margit signs to me and says I should get ready in two minutes because we're going back to the Americans.

Suri is the leader and besides we might well get home sooner from there. I'm not going without Ilonka, I say, and Ila won't leave the rest of the group, what can I do, there's no time to think, the vehicle is off and Margit is gone. It hurt a lot, I was very sad. Especially when a few people remarked, so this is what has become of all her friendship, she's gone just the same. Well, I had to admit I was disappointed in both Gitta and Margit. I thought we'd stay together till the end, but they didn't want to. Later I forgave them, only then I missed them very much.

We spent the next few days making preparations, or rather with the possibility that we could get a place on a vehicle where we had no right to a place, because it didn't come for us. But we managed it just the same and a journey by road followed, Anten, Carlja, Dallin, Postlin, Karlstadt, Perlenburg, Pritzwalk, Retzin, terrible devastation, we can see nothing but ruins now, this isn't the sort of journey you dream about. We have covered 200 kilometres in one day, I can't record the names of the towns, there are no more German signs, only Russian, and meanwhile we're looking for our bundles, someone else is sitting on them. Well at last at 9 o'clock in the evening they tell us to get off, we would look for somewhere to stay, but there's so much filth everywhere that we won't go anywhere like this in our own enlightened self-interest. At last we find a decent clean house, a German couple have found refuge there, I ask them to let nine people sleep here. We ask for hot water as well and they give us potatoes. What's more, some sort of buttermilk type of fluid, so we're going to have potato soup with soured cream. We have a good wash and I sleep on a divan, being an invalid.

In the morning we buy jam from the German and we give cigars in exchange. Honourable ladies decorated with the star that we are. You see he too has stolen the jam from the people who left it in the house. We get up at dawn, breakfast fit for a prince, vicious dog, we hurry to the truck. Pollak was there already, busy arranging things. Who was Pollak? He joined us in Grabow, dressed in Soviet military uniform, telling us that he had been only a little bit of a Nazi, he'd had to flee, now he'd like to return to Pozsony (Bratislava), he's willing to lead us home, we should give it to him in writing that we Hungarian deportees have asked him to do this, because we don't know our way around. He'll go to all the local agencies armed with this paper and we should request that they should put at his disposal the necessary vehicles, money and food aid. And so it was, he got something from everywhere, and it is thanks to him that we didn't starve to death. He got us to sign one more paper: when we got home we were each to send him 100 pengos. This however was not possible, because we didn't know his address, and besides, he disappeared in Pozsony. We signed both papers straightaway. First we take some water, it's nice weather, we're not sitting comfortably, because of Ilonka and Panni we all get told off for something. Never mind, this too will be over one day. We go through the town of Stettin, it's a terrible scene, they have made a thorough job of it, everything is gutted by fire, razed to the ground, it's good to see the ruins, but when are we going to get home, how are our families? It would be good to meet yorgy. We are told to get off the truck, we rest in a field, cook and wait for the train. So long as we don't have to spend the night here. It's a lovely sunny morning. We use bricks to cook maggi soup and potatoes, there's a bit of tinned food to go with it. It's getting hotter and hotter. We are baking, we keep circulating round the wagons, at last we climb into an open wagon in the usual way, first the luggage, then one of us gets in and loads it on, I find it very hard to climb up, but I don't want to be a burden to anyone, Ila does far more for me than I deserve, as it is, I'm on edge, I don't want to talk to anybody, I'm just forcing myself out of politeness. The heat is terrible, there must be a shower soon, and there is, Klari, Ilonka and I stay up in the wagon for the night. Thunder, lightning, it's hard to put up with a shower like this even in a closed space, let alone in an open wagon, with nothing on. We are having the time of our lives, you can imagine. Balin is the name of the place where we are standing. We don't leave the wagon in case anyone should take our places, we suffer like this till noon the next day. Lots more people get in, up to now we thought there wasn't even room for a pin. Some men are getting on as well, Poles, they keep stuffing themselves with good food. There's an ill-natured Polish woman sitting next to me, she and her companion never stop eating and smoking. By popular request the Polish Jewish men sing Kol Nidrei and Yiddishe Mamma.

It's sad, many people are crying, I don't like sadness. At last we're off, the first station is Schonfeld, then a lot of small stations, then Garskow, Neuenbruck, Paryten. The Polish woman is stuffing herself with tinned liver, but she doesn't offer any to anyone else, unfortunately we haven't got anything to eat. Everyone's eating, even the women from our lager, where did we go wrong, after all we did get ourselves bread and jam. We get to Stargart, some awful people get on, the great heavy sacks they throw land on our heads, shoulders, eyes, the dirty Russian czars. Up to now we haven't managed to catch anything, now we'll get lice. Jutka and Anci get squeezed out, we too can hardly breathe. Olitz is the next town, Harintzwald, it's beautiful, picturesque, we're getting near to Poland, the turmoil gets worse, we're going to suffocate. I have heard that a lot of people have in fact died on the way home. I wouldn't like to give them that pleasure. Just let me get home, I'll get better and I'm not going to anyone deport me. The others indicate their agreement. Awful devastation, dirt, filth everywhere.

Zohlhelsdorf is the name of the station where we are stopping. Kolbin is next. I've just heard from one of the Poles that Germany surrendered on May 8th Tutz is next. The Polish woman is eating cottage cheese, we've had nothing since yesterday. If only they'd give us something but they are not taking care of us at all. It would be good to know where Pollak is, I expect he's wandered off to somewhere where there's good food. Dirty men with beards are still jumping on top of us. What's going to happen, now it's raining as well. We can all get under my brown blanket. Nobody knows anything, we're in a state of complete uncertainty. Someone is shouting into the wagon from time to time, we can't see him, because we can't even move. So this is what he is shouting: Listen to me Hungarians, I'm coming back soon, and I'll tell you everything. Of course he doesn't come back and we still don't know anything.

The wagon keeps on going into the unknown. The next station is Blomberg. I'm not too interested any more. The wait has been too long, getting home too far away. The crowd is getting off somewhere, we follow, we shouldn't have, we'd go back, but we can't. We're in a right mess. It's a big station, we can't go again till 10 o'clock. I wouldn't like to be seen by anyone. We're a wretched lot with our bundles, can anyone really be waiting for us at home?

We get on again and then off again, we don't know how many times we've got off then got on again. People are coming and going, the Russians stare at us – they chase us away – there's no place for us anywhere, it's enough to make us despair. I can hardly drag myself along, my poor bit of baggage is dreadfully heavy and I don't want anyone to carry it for me, after all, everyone's got their own problems, we get in, we go, we get off. Klari is busy with the cooking. Inocecovna is the name of the station, I don't even feel like writing any more, we're going again soon any way, we get off again, they give out soup, we take some, it's awful. It's a big town, you can sell anything, I want to sell my white pique blanket for bread, but I can't get any, there's none left. Klari does an exchange, my white silk blouse which I got from Margit turns into bread. And now, what's going to become of us. We are going to Posen, someone says, the Red Cross there will take care of us. We're all at the end of our tether, I too am really suffering. Pollak, what's going to happen? He's running about here there and everywhere, he can't achieve anything, we get on a little train, we pass through several small stations, filth everywhere, Gerzo, then we get to Ternovac, we've been travelling for two days and two nights, we're in a terrible state. There's no one to guide us, it's cold, it's dark, Ostrogovsk is another station in between. We sleep in some barracks, you don't know who's going to step on your bed or when. The dressing on my leg hasn't been changed for five days, it hurts like hell. We get up at five after sleeping in the open, it's good to move on. The station building is big, it's been bombed, lots of Russians, Ukrainians, only 200 Hungarians. That's quite enough, because they are shouting as if everybody was deaf. Pushing and jostling as we get on, everyone is thinking only of themselves, you can see here how selfish people are. At last we get on, lots of men, any politeness is out of the question, if they could everyone would kill the next person to get a place.

The wagon arrives at Kattowitz. Civilisation, city life, confectionery, a cinema, a bank building, a flower shop, nobody marvels at us or feels sorry for us, we stop in front of a baker's, there is white bread in the window, we stare, nobody takes pity on us. We sit in the station building, it's raining, it's cold, I go to the Red Cross to get my dressing changed and to ask for bandages of some sort, in case anyone should need any on the way. They haven't got any bandages, but what does happen is that they get me a bed straightaway, saying that unless I am admitted straightaway my leg will have to be amputated, that's the state I'm in. I don't care, I say, I'm going home any way, I'm not staying in hospital. They bandage me up, I limp back to the others, I have to walk across half the city, I'm worried they might set off in the mean time and I'll get left behind. There are coffee houses, cinemas, cake shops on my way. A piece of cake would be nice, but we haven't got any money, only Ila has. She hands over all her money and we spend it on three big croissants sprinkled with sugar, and we even get 15 zlotys change. I take them back in good spirits together with Panni who's been sent with me to keep me company. Ilonka shared them out, everyone got a bite. We go on sitting around bereft of hope, there's a rumour they're going to take us to a lager, we'll have to stay there for a long time, because we need a transport to get away, and there aren't any just now.

The next minute there's a different rumour, and so on, till after about five more new rumours we get moving and get on the train that has come in the mean time. A lot of pushing and shoving, our nerves can't take the pace any more, people are crying, there are hysterical outbursts, complete panic. 28 kilometres from here there is some sort of station, there's a train for us from there, if we can make it to there. We clamber up with great difficulty and we succeed in leaving behind our bread bag, which also had in it Margit's scissors and my other silk blouse. They say we're going to have to walk a lot now, but we'll get nearer our goal. We get to Rybyl station after several smaller ones. It would be very good to be going home already, our patience and our endurance are running out, what's the point of carrying on. But at the end of the day I'm still in a hurry to get home to my dear ones. Perhaps we are not very far away now, although I haven't the foggiest where we are. I don't spend a lot of time with the others, I haven't got the patience to chat to them, I would rather speak to strangers, they might know more. An enormous bridge, blown up, we see the worst devastation here of our whole journey. Ratiber is the next place. The scene is terrible, it must have been an enormous city and there is not a single person left there, there are rats jumping about on the ruins, the station building is also completely bombed out, they've made a good job of it. There are Russians walking about the station, they don't so much as look at us. We want to sell our cigars, for my part I haven't got much at my disposal now, and I'm willing to give up what I have got for food. Unfortunately we've come to the wrong place. It's three or four days before a train or any sort of engine comes, what's to become of us.

Pollak too is helpless, because you can't get wagons from anyone. It would be a great pity for us to perish here, nobody would ever know where we were.

We're in the back of beyond. Dirty uncouth Russian soldiers, a few female soldiers. We were allocated shelter in one of the office buildings that was more or less in one piece, and we'd even got some heating going, but the Russians came and they wanted us to be with them for the night there. We managed to get away from their clutches, we ran away to an awful house where two men were already sleeping, they managed to reassure us that it was all right to sleep. It's sleeting, we cook maggi soup, we don't even feel like having it any more, it's dark. This is the worst stopping place of our journey so far, disgusting filth wherever we look, litter everywhere, human and animal remains that no one has bothered to clear away, if the good Lord helps us to get away from here, we are saved. We get up early in the morning, Ilonka brings me water to wash with from many kilometres away, even though she too is in bad shape already. We're waiting for something to happen.

We're hungry. Opposite the station we can see the ruins of a hotel, on the ground floor there are some sailors or railwaymen sitting at a table drinking. We venture in and ask for something to eat. They laugh at us. On our tour of reconnoitre we find the kitchen, with the door shut, we push it in and help ourselves liberally from a big tub of potatoes. Behind us there's a booming German voice. He shouts at us and takes the potatoes out of our hands. After prolonged pleading we come to an agreement. In exchange for cigars they give us potatoes and onions. We cook them and eat them. The news changes every five minutes, according to Pollak the only way we can get out of here is to do about 40 kilometres on foot. We are willing, but the others are not fit for the journey, so there are new plans, we are going, we are not going.

Russian soldiers are harassing us the whole time, only the good Lord saves us from them. Pollak thinks we should go back to Kattowitz, there will be a train for us there, or we should spend another night here and we'll still get some sort of transport. It is getting dark, it's pouring with rain, it's cold and our stomachs are empty. We're not staying here. We'd rather die. The Russians are buzzing round us all the time. Pollak behaves well, he looks after us. A military train has just arrived, Pollak arranges for it to take us, but where to?

We prepare to get on, where do you get on. The Russians are circling round us again. Pollak finds an escape route for us and going round the station building we found the wagons as well, it's pitch black and it's pouring with rain. There's a cold wind and we manage to stagger on to the wagons, which are stacked up with motorcycles, it doesn't matter, we sit down wherever we can find room on the motorcycles. Some people spent the night on a saddle, Ila and I in a basket, it was an awful torment, but it was still a good thing we didn't have to be with the Russians. After a long train journey we get back, they say the next station is Mahrisch Ostrau where there is a Red Cross centre with every comfort, e.g. bath facilities, food. This hope keeps us going, because we're having a dreadful night again, cold, hungry, etc. A railwayman takes pity on us and gives out some slices of bread. We get off again, get on, get off, get on, we've lost count how many times, we are at the end of our tether, and every step takes us nearer home. We're here at last. It's a big station, which has been bombed, nice roads, the mansions on them also bombed, the shops are closed. We see some mustard in a Meinl type shop, this is a bit of civilisation. We go on a long tram journey, but first Pollak shepherds us into a Red Cross centre where we get hot soup, and miracle of miracles, potatoes cooked in fat. You can queue up twice, and we do. After that we make for our lodgings by tram. Pollak makes arrangements on the tram too, we don't have to buy tickets, and at last we get off at a school where there are already masses of Haftlinge apart from us and they shout down to us that we'd have been better off not coming here, we've been sitting here for 8 weeks with no prospect at all of going home. We look at Pollak, he is helpless, but we go up just the same to the room allocated to us, there are beds. I share a bed with Ila, we sleep better this way, I don't even know how we are ever going to sleep without each other. I wonder where Margit and Gitta are, it was a shame not to stay together, I'm never going to forgive them.

They take us into a warm bath, then lunch and a rest. The 'Dudu', this is what they call the Red Cross here, behaves very well, we can queue up even three times and they don't say anything, they even give us cucumbers, this is food fit for human beings. There are a lot of people here, all sorts of nationalities, a veritable tower of Babel. After lunch we go back to the school. We have a rest, at 6 o'clock it's time to go for supper, but I don't go, lla brings me my share. We go to bed, we sleep in late in the morning, there is no Appel and we're not going further either. The weather is dismal, rainy and gloomy, in the courtyard they are teaching cadets to sing. It's getting on our nerves, hearing the same tune over and over again, they still can't learn it, we know it better already. Soon it will be time to go to the Dudu for food, it's nice and warm there, outside it's relentlessly dismal. It's cold and rainy. After lunch we go out in search of bread. The local people left here are very kind, they have pity on us and they give us bread, jam and margarine too. We manage to get shoes for lla, and we manage to get a whole loaf of bread. We're all right for a while now. I hope it's going to last us till we get home. I'm an incorrigible optimist, I soon see myself at home. In the evening they give out soup again.

I'd like to eat something other than soup already. Ila is not well, I take her to hospital. Her heart is very bad. What's going to happen, if she can't go on, I'll stay with her. I'm not going to leave her. Don't worry dear Ila, we'll get home.

Women we don't know join us, I suppose it's because we're in such good condition. Nebbich. Well, come on then. In the evening we set off again, we go across a bridge at some point. 'Without a sound,' says Pollak. We're deaf, blind and dumb; hungry more than anything else. Pollak is a decent fellow, he promises we'll get home, but he gets us to sign a form. Each of us is to send him 100 pengos when we get home. That's all right with us, we sign, we just wish we were home already. Where are we? Pozsony, Ligetujfalu. A suburb.

Rather damaged. We go in. They speak to us nicely, in Hungarian. They saw me writing, they think I'm a journalist. They offer me some cheese 'susza', I eat it, I bring it up again.

Brr. We can see a little restaurant of sorts. What is to be had? Potatoes with fried eggs. O.K. This stayed down.

They direct us to the Red Cross. Pollak has disappeared. Why? Sharing a room with men. They put me in the hospital. No chance. We're certainly not staying here. We go to the basement. At least we'll be on our own. Ilonka mentions her brother who is a doctor, we get a plate of pasta. It isn't very much. At lunch time they give out soup. I am not really interested any more.

In the office you can get 300 Czech krones, or 100 Hungarian forints. We choose the latter. They are selling cherries in the street, I daren't break into the money in case it is needed at home, even though I wouldn't mind eating some. When I get home I'll eat fruit by the kilo. A woman speaks to me, I remind her of someone. My sister, I say, lives at Suto u.2, that's where we were together. She also lived there. I ask her, should she get home first, to be sure to let my family know. She didn't do it. She's a bad person. We go to the railway station three times, we still can't get on a train. We saunter back, dispirited. At the fourth attempt we succeed, we travel by night, the air is thick, we're at the end of our strength. Everyone is on edge. Day is breaking. What can we see? The zoo, a railway bridge, the nyugati palyaudvar railway station. Ila and I have arrived.

Appendix 2: Budapest 1945 to 1956
(This is the memoire of Mary Chait, Judy Rona's daughter, including their escape from Budapest in 1956).

The liberation, when it finally came, was in most cases not everything Mami and Apu and people like them had hoped for and dreamed about. Conditions were chaotic, transport erratic, food was short and many people preoccupied with their own problems. In addition there was some antisemitism to be found among the ranks of the victorious Allies. I had noticed before that the newsreels about the liberation of the concentration camps never mentioned that most of the victims were Jews, but I was still astounded to discover recently from a radio programme that this omission was in fact a deliberate policy.

One of the group of women Mami was with in Boizenburg (NB In August 1944, the SS set up a Neuengamme satellite camp for women in Boizenburg. 400 Jewish women from Hungary were transported from Auschwitz-Birkenau to Boizenburg. They had to work 12-hour shifts, day and night, for the company Thomsen & Co., producing and repairing parts for fighter planes and warships. The Boizenburg satellite camp was probably evacuated on 28th April 1945 ahead of the advancing Allied troops. The women were forced to march in the direction of Neustadt-Glewe. On 2nd May 1945, the prisoners were liberated near Groß-Laasch by the US Army.) I kept a journal of their liberation and journey home and Mami received a typewritten copy of the journal in September 1965 from Klara, another member of the group. I had always assumed this Klara was Klari Vertes, a friend of Mami's still living in Budapest, but when I asked Klari Vertes about the journal she said she hadn't been with Mami in the war, so the Klara who sent the journal must be someone different, and the note accompanying the copy of the journal gives a no further clues to her identity. I read some of the journal when it came, but I wish now I had read it more thoroughly and discussed it with Mami. I asked Apu if he knew where the journal was after Mami's death, but I finally found it among other memorabilia in the house when he too died.

The tale told by the journal is appalling. More often than not Mami and the others had to fend for themselves, fighting for food and shelter. They were forever waiting for the next transport to leave. Although so much of their time was spent waiting around they never dared to relax: they were constantly anxious a transport might leave without them. When they did manage to get on a transport, a truck or some wagons, it was usually overcrowded and very uncomfortable, nor did they have any real idea where they were in fact going. There were always rumours going round, followed by counter rumours. No one ever knew anything for certain. At first the women kept their hopes up and maintained a positive attitude despite setbacks, but they were gradually reaching the end of their strength and their patience. Even the weather and the scenery they passed through seemed to reflect their mood. At first the diarist writes about lilacs blossoming and some beautiful sunny days, although she does talk about pouring rain and devastation as well. Later all we read about is cold, rain, ruins and filth everywhere and fellow passengers who are dirty, uncouth and selfish. All the women wanted was to get home in the hope of finding loved ones who had also survived, even Mami, who knew she was very unlikely to find any of her immediate family alive. On one occasion the diarist was told that her bad leg would have to be amputated unless she agreed to be hospitalised at once, but even this threat was not enough to detain her. The women were in a bad state of health, and this was is not the only occasion when one or other of them was advised to be cared for in hospital. At other times they had trouble getting any medical care at all.

The journal begins on 28 April 1945, the night before the camp was evacuated. After being on the march for five days the prisoners were liberated by the American 82nd Division under Major-General James M. Gavin on 2nd May. According to the journal, the moments of liberation itself was not altogether clear: the German camp personnel carried on leading them to the destination they had been given by the first Americans who stopped them at a crossroads and some of the Germans stayed on with the prisoners for a few days. In all this time there seems to have been a subtle shift in the relations between the prisoners and their guards, although some of the guards were still behaving exactly as they had done before. The Kommandant, who had been appointed to his post only a few weeks before, does seem to have wanted to look after the prisoners and on hand them over to the Americans in an orderly fashion.

It had been decided at Yalta that Hungary was to be in the Soviet sphere of influence, so the Americans passed on the Hungarian deportees to the Russians stationed at Grabow. At Grabow Mami's group acquired an unofficial guide called Pollak. Pollak had had to flee from his home in Pozsony (now Bratislava) at the time of the liberation because he had been just a little bit of a Nazi sympathiser.

He felt that guiding the deportees home and helping them to obtain food and shelter on the way would be his own ticket home. He got all the women to sign a piece of paper requesting him to help them get home and authorising him to apply to the appropriate agencies for food, transport and other facilities on their behalf. They also had to sign that they would later pay him for his services. The writer of the journal does acknowledge that they would probably have starved to death without him and on one occasion he managed to get them so away from Russian soldiers who had designs on them. He negotiated free rides on the tram in one place and sometimes knew where to find Red Cross centres to take care of them. There were other occasions when he too was at a loss what to do next. He disappeared when the group finally reached Pozsony.

It is amazing to me how the diarist found the energy to keep a journal in those circumstances. She records that they lost track of how many times they got on and off various trains. She did note down the names of many of the places they passed through many of them will have different names now and perhaps some are too small to appear on most maps. I have been able to find Stargard on the map, the place where the diarist says Mami and her friend Anci were squashed off a train by new people getting on. This incident is only mentioned briefly, so I presume they managed to get back on again. The diarist probably lost track of time too, because the only dated entry in the journal is the one right at the beginning, although she also mentions that when their train was passing through Tutz they learned that Germany had surrendered on 8 May. It certainly sounds as if the journey took several weeks.

The final leg of the journey was from Pozsony to Budapest. The women went to the railway station four times before they managed to get on a train. They travelled through the night, wondering the whole time if they really were going to arrive in Budapest. As day was breaking they looked out of the window anxiously to see the zoo on the outskirts of Budapest, followed by a railway bridge and then recognised the nyugati palyaudvar railway station. The final words of the journal are "Ilaval hazaerkeztunk", lla and I have arrived home. I find these words deeply moving, no matter how many times I read them. I try to imagine how Mami must have felt at that moment.

Mami must have planned out well beforehand what to do next. She knew that her friends the Zadors had escaped at the Monor railway station, so she went straight to their house in Kispest hoping to find them there. They were overjoyed to see her and welcomed her into their home where she was to stay for the next year. They helped her on the road to recovery: they had been friends before and their close bond that now developed between them continued all their lives. Erzsi found out about her mother's last few days from Mami and they exchanged stories of what they had been through. The Zadors adventures had also not finished with the liberation: a Russian officer, although Jewish himself, didn't believe Bandi when he claimed to be a Jew, because Bandi couldn't speak Yiddish. As a result Bandi was taken away with other Hungarians to a labour camp before the family was finally reunited.

There is a photo of Mami taken in June 1945, which I think she needed for an identity card, that shows something of her physical and emotional state at this time. She was, however, determined to get back to normality and before long she opened up her parents' jewellery business to earn her livelihood.

Apart from the Zadors, Mami gradually re-established contact with other relatives and friends as well. Her cousin Mira had survived in a hiding in Hungary and Mami also had two uncles and an aunt in America. Her mother's youngest brother Marcus had kept in close touch with Mami's family even after leaving for America in 1925 and Mami kept the letter he wrote her in November 1945 as soon as it was possible to send letters from America to Europe. Szidi, Mira's mother, also wrote to Mami and I still have this letter too. Both Marcus and Szidi also sent parcels with food and clothing. Peter Schramm, Jakab Schramm's grandson survived and was taken first to France and then Israel by Youth Aliyah, but he later returned to Hungary because the Communist government didn't allow his mother to leave Hungary and join him in Israel. However, so far as I know, Mami had no contact with this branch of her family. On the Fernbach side the only person left alive for Mami to stay in touchwith was Bozsi, the widow of her uncle Vilmos Fernbach. Bozsi later married another jeweller, Jozsi Gabor.

One day Mami saw Apu in the street. Her heart beat faster, but she didn't go up to him or talk to him. Apu had a half share in a property in Kispest he had bought with Imre and when he went to look at the house he also called on the Zadors to see what fate had befallen them. (I have already mentioned that the Zadors were friends of Apu's family too.) Apu had already ascertained that in Rakosszentmihaly only a handful of Jews were left of a community of several hundreds. The Zadors were pleased to see him and said he should go and see Mami, who was working in her shop. He told me more than once the words he spoke to Mami on this occasion: "Most mar sohase engedjuk el egymas kezet" "From now on were never going to let go of each other's hand".

Apu had been liberated earlier than Mami, on 20 December. Budapest was then still under German occupation, so he could not go straight home, but had to wait until the beginning of February. He had two stories to tell about the days just before liberation. One was a memory of waking up feeling lovely and warm one morning said after sleeping in a school courtyard; the reason was a layer of thick snow which had fallen overnight and provided an extra layer on top of his blanket. The other story concerned one of his comrades who was a wealthy man and bribed the officers to let him sleep in a place where he thought he would be safe from the Allied bombing raids: despite this precaution this man was the only person in the camp to die in one of these raids.

On the day of his liberation Apu was not well and had not gone to work. The Russian officers would not let anyone back into the barracks where Apu had left his coat. Apu lost not only his coat, but also the last letter he had got from his father, which had been in his coat pocket. Presumably the Russians wanted to loot the barracks. There was a great deal of looting going on. Some Russians ordered Apu to take the boots off some dead people, but Apu refused. On another occasion Apu was ordered to load the contents of a shop on to a truck. Realising that the soldiers would not want to leave any witnesses to their looting alive, Apu escaped through the back door of the shop.

As the Russian liberators and the Hungarians were not always on the best of terms, Apu learnt the Russian for "I am Jewish", but was later advised that this declaration would not necessarily help him with the conquerors.

There was a great deal of bitterness and settling of scores going on, but Apu refused to join in when invited to go and take revenge on Nazi sympathisers. He was aware that innocent people could become victims of this type of rough justice, which could also result in permanent injuries for those attacked.

It did not take long for Apu's flair for business to kick in. On his way home he found lying in the road an abandoned horse saddle and other horse riding equipment, which he exchanged for a tub of fat. There was a tremendous shortage of food, and Apus next deal was with cabbages. He saw a farmer bringing a truckful of them into Budapest, obviously wanting to sell them, and Apu immediately saw an opportunity. He stopped the farmer, took him to a shop and acted as intermediary for the deal, taking a cut for himself. Apu also found a supplier of canvas for a lady who wanted some for the Bulgarian army. It was Apu's uncle Ire who introduced him to the lady in question and Apu did not realise Imre expected a cut, so this created some bad feeling between them. To replace the coat he had lost on the day of his liberation Apu now had one made of a hard wearing material called Loden, and he gained a reputation for always having some money in the pocket of this coat. Eventually he became a partner in Lakos, Szekely es Fenyves, a retail outlet for textiles situated in Petofi Sandor utca in the smart shopping centre of Budapest.

Despite these successes Apu felt the shortage of food together with the other inhabitants of the capital city. On one occasion Vera offered him some bean soup when Apu was visiting them. Apu declined, knowing it was too precious to give away. The offer and refusal were repeated several times and later Apu said that he would have accepted the offer, had it been repeated just one extra time.

Apu had been very happy to find Vera, Pista and their mother Aranka still alive. Pista had already made his mind up that he wanted to leave Hungary eventually, and the Joint Distribution Committee would have provided the means for him to do so straightaway, but he felt it would be wrong to leave his mother and sister on their own at this point. Vera carried on the family business while Pista decided to study mechanical engineering. Other Kallos relatives that Apu re-established contact with were his uncle Imre that he had always been close to, his cousin Zsuzsa Szende, daughter of Sari, and Eva Kallos, daughter of Nandor and Teri. Apu and the rest of the family found Eva, a young girl at this time, hard to get on with and eventually lost touch with her. Apu later found no out what had happened to her: she married twice; her first husband was a soldier with whom she had two children, a boy and a girl and her second husband was a journalist who used to drink and was violent to her. Eva died of Parkinsons Disease in 1986 at the age of 56.

Apu was also in touch with his aunt Hermine in London, who told him she had heard about a Rona who had escaped to Switzerland, who could be Erzsike. Apu felt a little jealous about that possibility, he felt that his sister had managed things better than him, not for the first time. He found out later that Erzsike had in fact died in Belsen, just weeks before the war was over.

When Apu went back to his parents' house he had the task of digging up the whole garden to find some hidden treasure, entrusted to Simon by the second wife of Aranka Einzig's husband. Aranka was a sister of Apu's mother and had died young. If you lived in a flat, as many people did, one option to keep your valuables safe was to ask friends or family with a garden to hide them for you. Simon had wanted Apu to know where he was hiding the valuables and shouted out, Look it Laci, this is where I'm putting them. Apu got very annoyed at the way his father was telling the whole world and went off without looking. Because of this he now had no idea where to start. With Pista's help he did eventually find the box and handed it over to the lady concerned. After checking through it she remarked that one small item was missing. She probably didn't realise how lucky she was to get her hoard back at all not everyone who hid other people's valuables returned them to the rightful owners.

Apu had plenty to tell Mami about when he met her again. She had other suitors as well, but rejected them in favour of Apu. She told me one consideration for her was that she could not contemplate marrying anyone who had not known her family. She agreed to marry Apu, but wanted to delay the wedding for a few months.

Apu had been baptised while in the forced labour service, together with all the rest of the camp, as previously mentioned. He insisted that Mami should follow his example, so that their future children would not suffer as they had done. The way he put it to me was that he could see no point in continuing to be hated, reviled, persecuted and killed for a set of beliefs he did not subscribe to in any case. Mami was reluctant, particularly because she knew that the children of baptised Jews often turned out to be antisemitic. She acceded to Apus wishes but drew the line at attending the conversion classes that led to the baptism. Most of my parents' circle took this path: nor was it a new phenomenon by any manner of means a substantial number of assimilated Jews in Germany and the Austro-Hungarian Empire had been getting baptised for over a hundred years prior to this. I don't think anyone brought up in postwar Britain or America can truly put themselves in the position of those who took this step.

The marriage took place at a Budapest registry office on 25 May 1946, with Apu's uncle Imre and Mami's brother-in-law Jancsi Halasz as witnesses. There are no wedding photos: it must have been a quiet affair and they must have both felt the absence of their closest family. Mami prepared the celebratory dinner herself, and she complained to me that Apu had been late arriving, a sign of things to come! Afterwards Mami and Apu went on honeymoon by Lake Balaton.

There was a shortage of accommodation, but Mami and Apu found a flat to rent on the 4th floor at no. 3 Hegedus Gyula utca, which they both liked immediately. The flat had two rooms, and regulations stipulated that a flat of this size had to be occupied by at least two persons. For this reason Mami had also given it as her address when applying for the marriage papers, although it was only Apu who had moved in before the wedding. The registrar made the remark I see you are living together already. Apu wanted to use the furniture his father had given to his sister Erzsike when she got married and he went to Tab to collect it a few days before the wedding. There was only one train a day to Tab and Apu had already missed it two days running, so he decided to walk to Siofok, which is on the way to Tab. He described that day to me as the happiest day of his life. As he walked he kept thinking to himself, Just a few more days and she'll be mine. Apu told me many times that in his whole life he never thought of marrying anyone else.

So Mami and Apu embarked on their married life together, which was to last for forty-six years, until Mami's death in 1992.

October 1956 was a turning point in the life of our family and many others. The uprising against Soviet Communist rule that started on 23 October in Hungary is regarded by many historians as a milestone presaging the collapse of the USSR three decades later. Stalin had died in 1953 and his successor Nikita Khruschev had started talking about reforms, preparing the ground for repressed discontent to come to the surface and bubble over. The Hungarian uprising started as a student demonstration in sympathy with a strike in Poland, another Soviet satellite. The students were joined by large numbers of their fellow countrymen, patriotic poems were read out and they demanded to speak on the radio. Shots were fired, but many of the police and the military joined the demonstrators and Imre Nagy, a moderate Communist, was swept into power by popular demand. When under pressure from the masses he demanded the removal of Soviet troops, threatened to leave the Warsaw Pact and to introduce multi-party government, the Kremlin decided to take action and Russian tanks rolled into Hungary on 4 November, swiftly crushing the uprising.

I could tell something was in the air as I came home from school on the afternoon of Tuesday 23 October. By the next morning we could hear the sound of shooting in the street and there was no question of going to school. Even Apu stayed at home. I remember Mami telling him off for going out on the balcony to see what was happening – she told him it was irresponsible of him to put himself in danger from a stray bullet. On the Thursday the fighting must have intensified because we took shelter in the cellar of our building for a few hours.

The new radio Apu had bought just a short time before came in very handy. We were able to listen to Radio Free Europe and the BBC as well as the Hungarian stations. I remember the announcer introducing a speech by Imre Nagy 'Nagy Imre nyilatkozik'. We spent much of the time glued to the radio.

My parents had mixed feelings about the uprising. They were in sympathy with its aims, but at the same time the Communists had repressed antisemitism along with everything else: most Jewish people were afraid of a resurgence of anti-Jewish feeling, particularly as some of the top Communists had been Jews. I didn't know anything about it at the time, but on our visit to Hungary in August 2002 Marsi told me that some of the residents of our building had made threatening remarks to Mami.

It was a confusing time for me. I had already had some inkling that not everyone thought the Communist regime was as marvellous as we had been led to believe at school and now it was quite hard to work out who were the goodies and who the baddies. In the heyday of the uprising we had seen people smashing up a big five pointed Communist star on a nearby building; out on the street again a few days later I caused considerable consternation to Mami when I asked her in a loud voice if they had finished knocking it down yet – by that time the Communists had taken control again.

It was common knowledge that thousands of refugees were pouring over the border to Austria and there were a lot of discussions taking place in our flat on this subject. Apu was determined to seize this opportunity to leave Hungary. A young man from the floor below us had some contacts and Pista too was making plans. The Communist government reinstated by the Soviet army promised to give exit visas to anyone who wanted to leave, but Apu didn't trust them. Mami would have preferred to wait for official papers, but Apu overruled her, remembering that she had once before vetoed plans to leave the country. In the event the government did honour their promise to grant exit visas to those who wanted to go and those who left later with official papers were able to take more of their possessions with them. Perhaps those who wielded power wanted to get rid of the discontents to forestall future unrest. This may explain why crossing the border to Austria illegally was also relatively easy, apart from the fact that some of the border guards might have wanted to turn a blind eye of their own accord. Had Apu been able to gaze into a crystal ball he would have waited: in the absence of such supernatural powers he was not prepared to take any chances. The reasons for leaving now were more pressing than in 1948 when the State of Israel had been declared. Not only had we experienced eight years of living in fear under Communism, but we had also used up our money with no prospects of being able to make any more. Apu was essentially a businessman and private enterprise was forbidden. His monthly salary was scarcely enough to buy food for a few days. In addition it was plain that there was still a great deal of antisemitism and as a result of the Holocaust Mami and Apu had no elderly parents or other close family ties to keep them in Hungary, unlike many other people who would have liked to leave. A lot of the people my parents felt closest to left around this time, some before and some after us. Perhaps in modern parlance we would have been classed more as economic migrants than asylum seekers, but there was much more to the decision to leave than economic considerations just the same.

During the uprising we received a telegram expressing concern for us from Apu's cousin Josephine in Brentwood and we already had the letter of invitation from Aunt Hermine, so Britain was the obvious place to go, although the possibility of Israel came up again. Mami had relatives in America, but I don't remember America being discussed as a possible destination. Apu's short-lived membership of the Communist party might have been an obstacle to being granted entry into the USA and perhaps Apu was happier to rely on his own relatives for help and support than to depend on Mami's relations for any succour. Britain was greatly respected in Hungary and Apu was sure it was a good country to live in. He never regretted his choice in later years. Pista, who was younger, was equally sure that Canada was the country of the future and he too has never regretted his decision. He had first made up his mind he wanted to live in Canada when the Canadian hockey team visited Hungary before the war. Many other Hungarians, both Jewish and non-Jewish, opted for Australia. Most people chose a country where they had relatives, friends or other contacts who would help them to obtain entry permits and offer them guidance and support as they started life in their new home. Apu's second cousin Sanyi Rona went with his family to Paris, where his wife Jolan had relatives, but Sanyi's niece, Agi Ferber, as well as Mami's cousin Mira stayed in Hungary because of family responsibilities to elderly parents. Altogether 200,000 people left Hungary in this period, about ten percent of them Jewish. Many western countries were sympathetic towards the Hungarians and the uprising, so they were willing to take in the refugees.

While all these discussions were going on, I was not at all sure I wanted us to leave behind everything familiar and remember thinking that if we did go I would at least take my new doll. The funny thing is that I don't remember at all what happened about the doll. Perhaps I forgot all about it when the plans for leaving turned into reality. Two things have stuck in my mind about the night before we left. One was that Mami showed me how to make the sign of the cross, which might be important in Catholic Austria if we were to keep our Jewish origins secret. Religion, which had not mattered under the Communist regime in Hungary, would now become a more important issue in our lives. I felt more anxious about my Jewish background than if we had been openly Jewish – although I don't think I could have put it into words, I think what I felt was that if it was important to hide our origins, being Jewish must still be dangerous. My second memory of our last night in our flat was looking at the glass panelled door to the hall from my bed and trying to imagine that I would never see that door or the rest of our flat again. When it comes to saying good-bye to what we feel inside is a permanent part of our life, it is hard to take in what we know with our reason to be true. I remember having the same feeling much more recently when Apu had just died in the Royal Free Hospital in London and the nurses left me alone with him. I said half aloud to myself that I would never see him again to try overcome the feeling of unreality, but you never can quite, however many times you have experienced this strange dichotomy.

To pay for the guide who was going to take us across the border, Apu had had to borrow money from Marsi, who later got her money back from our friends the Zadors. The Zadors left for Switzerland eventually, but they waited for the official papers. Apu had also arranged to hand our flat over to Marsi's sister Annus and her family: he gave them advice on how to receive authorisation to keep the flat – another family was also interested in it.

On the morning of December 15 Marsi accompanied us to the Keleti Palyaudvar railway station where we were to catch the train to Gyor. We had hardly walked a few steps away from our building when a limousine stopped by us, asked us where we were going, and gave us a lift to our destination. When the car first stopped Mami and Apu thought they were going to arrest us. Limousines of this sort were normally used by important government officials and the like. Perhaps the occupants of the car did guess what the purpose of our journey might be, but decided to turn a blind eye. I know that at another point in our journey, I'm not sure exactly when, a soldier, policeman or border guard told Mami not to be afraid, he wasn't afraid. Having got to the station it was discovered that I had left behind my watch, which was some sort of family heirloom – the faithful Marsi ran back to the flat to collect it and got back to the station in time to wave us off.

In Gyor we met our guide and the rest of the group he was taking across the border that day. I have wondered since if it occurred to Apu that our route out of Hungary was through the area where our Reichenfeld ancestors had first settled some two centuries previously and where they had continued to live for several generations. My guess is that his mind was more on our present situation – would we get to Austria safely, what would happen next if and when we did, how would we go on to Britain. Many years later I saw a film about a Jewish boy preparing to make for the border as we did. In the film, the boy recited the traditional prayer for going on a journey with his grandfather. My parents would not have thought of praying, but the prayer expresses very well the hopes and fears that must have been in their minds:

'May it be your will, Lord our God and God of our fathers, to conduct us in peace, to direct our steps in peace, to uphold us in peace, and to lead us in life, joy and peace to the haven of our desire. Deliver us from every enemy, ambush and hurt by the way, and from all afflictions that visit and trouble the world. Send a blessing on the work of our hands. Let us obtain grace, loving kindness and mercy in your eyes and in the eyes of all who behold us.'

When everyone had assembled we got on another train. One of my classmates was also on the train and I asked my parents if her family were absconding as well. It did not occur to me to keep my voice down, so I was shushed, but there were no untoward consequences. The plan was that as the train was getting near the border we would transfer from the passenger carriages to the part of the train made up of goods trucks. We were supposed to do this at a scheduled stop, but Mami got off prematurely with Raymond when the train was waiting at signals or something similar. Apu was dismayed when the train started up again and shouted out for it to stop so they could get back on again. Strangely enough I don't recall this incident at all and only know about it from my parents. We did eventually get into the goods trucks – for Mami certainly not a new experience.

By the time we got off the train at Hegyko, darkness had fallen. From here we had to go on foot to the shore of Lake Fertu (known as the Neusiedlersee on the Austrian side) where two boats were waiting to take us across the lake to the other side of the border. Apu was carrying Raymond as well as luggage: it was all getting too heavy for him and he ended up ditching one of the cases he had been carrying. I wonder if anyone found it and made good use of whatever we had in it. Mami, for her part, twisted her ankle and had to lean on me for the rest of the trek. When we finally reached the boats, we found the Russians had shot holes into them, so that people had to take turns to bail out the water coming in through them. Another problem was that when we had got into the boats it was found that there were too many people in the boat our family had chosen to get into. The guides said two people would have to get out and move to the other boat. No-one would budge, everyone was in family groups. Apu broke the stalemate by agreeing to get into the other boat with me. I think I went to sleep on Apu's arm. There was a thick mist and it took us six hours to find what we hoped was the right spot on the Austrian side. A bonfire was lit and eventually we were spotted and taken to a refugee camp near Eisenstadt. Almost immediately I started being sick and was taken to a hospital in the town. There was no physical cause for my sickness, it was more due to my emotional state after our adventures. It was while I was being sick that I tasted my first banana - tropical fruit that would have had to be imported had not been available in Hungary. I could not keep the banana down and have never been able to eat bananas since. In the hospital I received a package that had been prepared by the WVS: it contained a handkerchief, a ball-point pen and a pad of paper among other things. I also got a pair of booties from somewhere – I think the shoes I had been wearing had been done in on our long walk to the boats. I was at an impressionable age and have always remembered this rather low point in our lives, when we were dependent on others for the basics of existence, with hardly anything we could call our own. You can have a secure existence one minute and the next find yourself a refugee in need of food and shelter – it isn't something that only happens to other people and refugees are not a strange alien species.

I remember going for a walk round Eisenstadt with Apu and noticing the signs of western affluence with all sort of exotic goods on sale. It was also on this walk that Apu told me one of the best things about our future life in Britain would be that there nobody knew we were Jewish and we would be able to start a completely new life.

Pista, who had gone before us and was already in Vienna, somehow found out where we were and came to the camp to find us. An announcement was made over the camp loudspeaker for Apu and Mami to go and meet him and he took us back to Vienna, for which we needed the written sanction of the authorities. Pista had already been joined by his fiancee Agi. In Vienna we stayed in what I thought was a hotel at the time, but have since found out was a house of ill repute which had been put at the disposal of the refugees. Apparently I had not stopped being sick – Agi says I was sick all over her bed. However in Vienna it was Raymond's turn to be ill: he ran up a high temperature and was treated by an Austrian doctor. Mami was stuck in with him, but managed to get out for long enough to acquire a top made of a new fabric called nylon – a turquoise jumper with three quarter length sleeves. We were thrilled to have escaped from Communist austerity and to be in a free western environment where all sorts of weird and wonderful new products were available. Even now that the former Communist countries are no longer under the aegis of the USSR, I remember that we all breathed more easily after crossing the border from the Czech Republic into Germany on our recent European trip – from the moment the German border guards showed no interest whatsoever in looking at our passports, we felt we were back in western civilisation.

While in Vienna, Apu got in touch with his old boss Hugo Kemeny, who immediately offered him a job. Apu had no hesitation in refusing. He said Austria was far too near to Hungary and everything it represented – he was determined to stick to the original plan of going on to London, even though his prospects there were uncertain. Knowing how hard Apu found the first few years in Britain, I asked him once if he had ever regretted that decision. 'Never', he replied.

My parents visited the British Embassy in Vienna on December 21 to make arrangements to be admitted into Britain, armed with the visa they had been granted by the British consul in Budapest on 5 December, their Hungarian identity cards etc., all of which they had carefully packed. I still have the 'form of affidavit to be used in lieu of a passport' that they were each granted in Vienna. Apu declared that he was 'urgently desirous of travelling to the UK' in order 'to join my aunt in London.' The reason Mami gave was 'to accompany my husband', and the document also states that she in turn was accompanied by her named children. They both declared that they were unable to obtain a national passport or any form of document from the Government of the country in which they then resided. The back of the document is stamped with a number of imprints. From these we learn that the document is 'good for a single journey to the United Kingdom within three months from the date thereof', that the bearer must register at once with the police and that he or she may not enter employment without the consent of the Ministry of Labour and National Service. The documents were stamped again both by the Austrian police and the Immigration office at London Airport on 24 December. Apu's was stamped one more time, by the Aliens Registration Office on 27 December, and his National Insurance number is written on in pencil.

I don't know who paid for our tickets, but we flew to London Heathrow on 24 December from Vienna. The flight took six hours and we stopped briefly in Zurich. I was intrigued by the double decker bus that took us from the plane to the terminal, where Aunt Hermine was waiting for us. After going through the formalities we took a black London cab to her house in Kilburn.

Aunt Hermine had never met Mami before and when she saw how smart she looked, with her hair carefully done in an attractive style, she obviously came to the conclusion that she was the type of woman who spends all day painting her nails, because she told Mami that in Britain no-one goes to the hairdresser and everyone has to work, even the doctor's wife. My parents could never understand why Aunt Hermine rounded on Mami like that straightaway: they were both proud of her immaculate well-groomed appearance, and I don't think it occurred to them that it was possible to interpret it in a negative way - that this was what had caused Aunt Hermine to say what she did. I don't remember hearing Aunt Hermine's remarks, but the story was repeated to me many times in later years and eventually I realised what was probably going on in our elderly relative's mind. Aunt Hermine was then 77, lonely, and no doubt embittered by much that had happened to her. It was unfortunate that her first impression of Mami was so mistaken. Mami worked just as hard at everything else as she did on her appearance. She looked like a film star and she always aimed for perfection in everything she did."

About the Author

Diana lives in London with her husband, Alex. They have four daughters. Now that she has retired from full time work she does a lot of travelling, singing, writing, and drawing. As a student she used to act (including on tour in the USA and at the Edinburgh Festival) but has not taken that up again, yet. Her career consisted of working as an international lawyer until she moved into international development where her focus is on peacebuilding, access to education and access to justice.

www.ingramcontent.com/pod-product-compliance
Lightning Source LLC
Chambersburg PA
CBHW050030090426
42735CB00021B/3431